To

Healing 12 a journey!

DIVORCE:
An
Uncommon Love Story

HEALING YOUR FAMILY
SAVING YOUR MONEY
AND
RENEWING YOUR LIFE

Blessings,
Dr. Marty

Dr. Marty Finkelstein

"Divorce: An Uncommon Love Story," by Dr. Marty Finkelstein. ISBN 978-1-60264-677-3.

Published 2010 by Virtualbookworm.com Publishing Inc., P.O. Box 9949, College Station, TX 77842, US. ©2010, Dr. Marty Finkelstein. All rights reserved. No part of this publication may be reproduced, stored in a retrieval system, or transmitted in any form or by any means, electronic, mechanical, recording or otherwise, without the prior written permission of Dr. Marty Finkelstein.

Manufactured in the United States of America.

SPECIAL THANKS TO:

Editor- **Jeanne Ballew** for her thoughtful editing and vision for this project.
Kiava Garnett for her computer expertise
Louis Leonardi for sharing the "fire walk."
Michael Norwood who from the beginning reminded me what my truth is, and who continued to inspire me to write this story, knowing how important this message was for everyone.
Steven Saul who always seems to be there in my life at the right moment.
Stu and Janna Zonder who created the healing space of music, and love to manifest and introduced me to my sweetheart.
David and Molly Finkelstein for being the best brother and sister in law, always there…
Lou Finkelstein my dad for being the best father who has never wavered in his love and commitment
Kathryn Lawson for her own healing and transformation that allowed this story to be shared.
Nathaniel and Julia Finkelstein who give me the blessing of being a dad. I am so proud of whom they are and the gifts they bring to the world.
My sweetheart **Julie Austin** who lights up my life with song and dance and always inspires me to be my best.

Other books by Dr. Marty Finkelstein

A Life of Wellness

If Relationships Were Like Sports, Men Would at Least Know The Score

8 Lessons of Life on Hole 1

The Seven Gifts

Moments in Time- CD of 15 original songs

This Book Is Dedicated To:

My Son, My Daughter, and
My Ex-Wife

and The Power of Healing and Love

FROM THE HEART

I truly have the best family ever. My whole life has been filled with support, guidance, lessons, and love. Not only have I been blessed with parents who have given me tools to go out into the world and live my dreams, I have parents who have shown me through their actions what is truly possible when it comes to relationships. They have demonstrated the unequivocal powers of unconditional love, trust, faith, and transformation. I feel honored and proud to share our story with the world.

Julia Finkelstein

The importance of acceptance and truth allows us to dive deeper beyond the common perceptions on marriage and divorce. This "uncommon love story" could turn out to be the greatest love story ever told. I have been blessed to have parents who continue to be an example of unconditional love and healing.

Nathaniel Finkelstein

An uncommon love story told by an uncommon man. Finkelstein bares his soul as he walks you through his journey from the emotional hell of divorce to expanded self awareness and subsequent success. This book should be mandatory reading for anyone applying for a marriage license. It's filled with real world wisdom you can only gain through years of experience. I've been married 26 years, and I couldn't put it down.

Steven Siebold, author of 177 Mental Toughness Secrets of The World Class

Reading Dr. Finkelstein's book is like having a friend share with you one of life's deepest experiences, and greatest secrets. Not just a transformative book for those going through divorce, but for anyone to discover a new way of handling conflict and staying love centered and in integrity amidst any of life's storms.

Dr. Michael Norwood, author of The 9 Insights of The Wealthy Soul

Table of Contents

INTRODUCTION

When I first got married I never imagined that I would eventually be writing a story about my divorce. In essence I do not believe my relationship ending was a conscious goal, yet choices, decisions, and actions throughout my marriage played their part in creating that outcome. I have come to realize that our actions and decisions can surprise us with astonishing delight, or surprise us with astonishing alarm.

If you ever have the opportunity to walk across hot coals, known as FIRE WALKING, just remember, don't stand on one spot to long, always continue walking with purposeful intent.

Many of my friends have requested I share this story to assist others across the fire called separation and divorce.

This is for anyone who desires to Heal Their Family, Save Their Money, and Renew Their Life.

Chapter 1:
Four Words That Feel
Like A Heart Attack

"I want a divorce," were the words that began a journey of pain, anger, and sadness that I did not want to take. It was a journey that evoked fears of the future and loss, riddled me with denial and confusion, and poked a hot branding iron into my heart, unleashing unwanted rage. Thankfully, it was also a journey of healing, discovery, and vulnerability that ultimately lead to forgiveness and love.

These types of journeys can only be taken alone. Even with the best of intentions on the part of family and friends, inevitably you are on your own to make decisions affecting all your relationships. This story is about that journey, the life lessons that I continue to learn, and the miracles that went well beyond what I could have possibly imagined when it began.

The words "I want a divorce," etched their way deep into my skin, muscles, and blood as if a cancer was rapidly taking over my body. I sat frozen for hours feeling like a victim, though truly I was not. My feelings were the result of having neglected the ongoing symptoms of an illness—symptoms that are simple to recognize when we are "awake." The harmony in the relationship that once existed was out of tune.

Where there was once affection and healthy communication, now there was judgment and isolation. Where there was once open-heartedness and trusting, now there was a feeling of being guarded and contracted. Where there was mutual admiration and sexual intimacy, now there was awkwardness and hopelessness. My partner and I once shared a mutual vision regarding family, careers, and spiritual development. Now the vision seemed clouded. Sadly, when we are sleepwalking through our relationship, symptoms are rationalized through denial and illusions until we are abruptly awakened.

Now I sat in disbelief. It was past midnight. Hours had passed. I was in total darkness, yet my wife's face kept being silhouetted through the corridors of my mind. I did not totally recognize her face since it offered no hope. It was cold and distant. It was a face I no longer could sweet talk or manipulate.

I finally managed to lift myself onto my wobbly legs and walked through the darkness into our bedroom. As I softly stepped forward, I could feel her presence as she slept. When I lifted my leg to take the next step, she jumped up from the bed screaming as if I had triggered her internal burglar alarm. I reacted by shouting that everything was okay and embraced her silently for about five minutes before she gently leaned away, climbed back into bed, and drifted back to sleep. As she did, I knew that nothing at the moment was okay.

Later I found out the true reason for her alarming scream. Somewhere in the mist of her disturbed dreams, she was startled by a sound and what she described as an ominous presence in the room. But it was not the fear of a stranger that woke her abruptly. It was the irrational fear that I was coming to kill her. It was hard to imagine that she could ever think I could commit such a horrific act, yet in what seemed like an instant, we had become strangers.

I hoped that sleep for me would be a pleasant escape. Maybe I would awaken and realize that all of this was simply a bad dream to capture my attention and truly wake me up to changes necessary to avoid the nightmare of divorce. I did not want to lose my family, yet it seemed that everything I had worked toward my whole life was being shattered. As much as I tried to get spiritually centered and feel faith in God, restless fear greeted me in the morning, exposing my emotional nakedness.

How Our Beliefs Affect Our Actions

When I first got married, I believed it was forever. My upbringing had instilled in me the belief that the family should never separate. Because of this belief, I probably would have remained in the trenches, attempting to save my children from the horrors of divorce, despite the difficulties my wife and I were having. At the time, it seemed better for my children to be brought up with a dysfunctional mom and dad rather than being raised with the scars from a broken family. I remembered feeling confused and scared as a child when my parents argued. I remembered praying in my room that my parents would not get divorced. I never wanted to have to make an emotional decision between my mother and father. Thankfully, I never had to.

My wife's experience, though, was very different than mine. As a little girl, she also observed the disenchantment between her mother and father, but she imagined that it might be best for her parents to separate and discover their true joy in life.

We have all had different childhood experiences, and our responses and reactions to those experiences easily shape the decisions we make later in life. There is not necessarily a right or wrong choice, yet it is important to discover within ourselves as we are healing and evolving where these initial impressions came from. My wife was clear that the time had come for a change. She felt that she was dying emotionally and spiritually, and that this was affecting her relationship with herself and our children. The choice of separation and divorce seemed like the only way for her to discover her authentic self again, feel alive, and to share her best qualities with our children. She had hoped our relationship would improve, but like a chronic illness, she had finally diagnosed it as terminal.

I Never Liked Roller Coasters

For the next several weeks, I was on an emotional roller coaster. The fear of losing my children and my wife consumed every breath with a pain that felt out of control. I remember one afternoon taking my children to see the movie, *Mrs. Doubtfire*, starring Robin Williams. He played a character who was being divorced by his wife and forced out of his home and away from his children by the courts. Nothing was more important to him than his relationship to his children. As we sat in the darkness of the theater, I cried silently as I related to his character. In one part of the movie, he explained to the judge that not allowing him to see his children would be like removing the air that he breathes. I deeply shared his sentiment. Though the movie dealt with the seriousness of divorce, Robin Williams showcased his incredible talent for humor by dressing up as a nanny so that he could spend more time with his children. My children laughed throughout the whole movie, not knowing that their mom and dad were having similar troubles, and that, if necessary, their dad would go to the same lengths to remain in their daily lives.

Willingness to Change

A weekend of transformation is exactly what I needed, and that is what the personal growth seminar had promised. I knew I needed help and new insights and ultimately to heal. We had still not shared our intentions with our children or family. I guess I believed there was still hope for our marriage. I knew that to enroll in this personal growth seminar I would have to be completely vulnerable and willing to share my deepest pains and fears. The very thought of this made me tremble inside.

I sat in the room with about 150 people. We were going to be with one another over the next three days from early morning until late evening. I gazed around the room anxiously as I realized that these strangers would soon know more about me than some of my closest friends. I had participated in seminars in the past, but this time was different. This time I was truly in pain. And the stakes were incredibly high with my family and my life being held hostage. I had hoped to discover over the next three days what it was about me that seemed to sabotage intimate relationships. And I hoped that if my wife saw my willingness to change that she might also see new possibilities for our marriage.

The first day went by quickly, and by the end of the evening, I felt a renewed sense of self. I had shared my story, and allowed my fears, sadness, and pain to be witnessed by the others in the room. Yet, the more exposed I was, the stronger and more alive I felt. The day was filled with insights, the type that make your hair stand on end and allow you to breathe deeper than you have breathed for awhile. I was beginning to believe that I could share my thoughts and feelings more clearly with my wife, but perhaps even more important, I could listen if she were willing to share her own pain regarding our relationship and separation.

Unexpected Revelations

When I awoke the next morning before setting off for the second day of my seminar, I turned and saw my wife on the other side of the bed—a bed that now had invisible borders separating us from each other yet still creating the illusion for our children that their mommy and daddy were together. I asked her if she would be willing to participate in a communication exercise with me before I left. She cautiously agreed and asked what was involved. She knew I was in a seminar, so she was not surprised by my unusual behavior. Here is how the exercise works. I asked her to share with me every way in which I had let her down, betrayed, or hurt her in our relationship. My promise was to listen attentively and openly and not to defend, respond, or rationalize anything that she shared. I would simply listen and ask "What else?" until she felt totally complete in sharing.

This was an amazing experience. When she shared a painful memory, I did say, "I am sorry," but other than that I gave her permission to express whatever painful experiences she desired that may have been suppressed for years. Throughout this, she shared moments of frustrations that I easily recalled and understood. There were other situations she mentioned that I simply did not remember. When she was done, I didn't ask her if she wanted to trade places and be the listener, nor did she volunteer. I saw how listening could create an intimate gift in a relationship. Until that moment, I had not realized my inability to truly hear my wife's thoughts and feelings. All day long at work, I skillfully and compassionately listen, yet sadly I had not developed those same skills in the most important intimate relationship in my life. So there we were now, face-to-face with a discomforting sorrow and an unpredictable future.

A few years later, I modified this exercise and integrated it in relationship workshops that I began leading. It provides an intimate paradigm for people to explore a new way of listening as well as getting in touch with what they truly feel deep inside. Imagine letting someone close to you share his or her wounded heart while you remain totally present, listening with compassion and without judgment. This can create a tremendous sense of freedom in any relationship if engaged in properly with a heartfelt purpose and a compassionate loving spirit.

Many people were in the seminar attempting to mend broken relationships. Some were with their spouses, others with children and parents. When one young man shared about his breakthrough with his wife, it seemed like a miracle. Yet the more I heard about others healing their relationships and discovering new beginnings, the more I felt rejected and hurt. My expectations and hope had me believe that if I were more willing to explore our marriage that somehow I would pass the test. Perhaps it wasn't a conscious test that she had created, but a test nonetheless. I imagined she thought I would be relieved and happy once she declared she wanted a divorce. If there was a test at that time, it only existed in my mind. Like a knight willing to slay the dragon to win the lady's hand, the illusions persisted, except that now it seemed too late.

At the end of the seminar, I did not have a wonderful story to share with the group. Instead of feeling empowered with new possibilities, I had failed. Though I felt I had given myself completely in this seminar with the most open and compassionate heart, crying more tears than I had cried my entire life, staring into the future I was still left with even a deeper fear for my children. I had played the best authentic emotional and spiritual game, and yet I had lost. I felt robbed.

An unexpected, wonderful revelation did occur, though, in the seminar. It was like the Rolling Stones' song, "You can't always get want you want, but if you try sometime, you just might find, you can get what you need." I got an insight related to my mother that opened the door to all my past intimate relationships with women. My mom had died several years earlier from cancer at the age of fifty-two. I was the younger son of two boys. For whatever reasons, I had always felt that my mother loved my brother more than she loved me. It was as if I was not good enough. Somewhere in the early emotional intelligence of a child, I determined that if my mother did not wholeheartedly accept me and love me, how in the world could anyone else? In contrast to these stored, confused feelings, I also knew I had a wonderful mom who was always there for me. Emotionally, I was entrenched with guilt before I even knew the meaning of guilt. As an adult, I realized that this childhood conflict of feeling unloved by my mom had carried over into my relationships with other women. If she couldn't love me unconditionally, how could any other woman?

Healing the Past by Changing the Present

There has been one constant in all of my intimate relationships . . . me. So as I observed my complex feelings during the seminar, I discovered how, to some degree, I had sabotaged all of my intimate romantic relationships. Somehow I would subconsciously manifest an end to the relationship with my girlfriends choosing to leave me. Perhaps initially it was the fear of deeper intimacy and commitment on my part. But, ultimately, it also was that I did not want to be the one who chose to leave the relationship. Because I did not feel that I deserved to be loved for who I was, I held back my own love and vulnerability. And I did this with my wife.

The magic of this insight and realization understood that I no longer had to be at the mercy of this belief. I was unveiling a secret that had been camouflaged in self-deception. But now the mirror from the past was no longer discolored, and I could see clearly. It felt like a hundred pound weight of lies had been lifted from my spirit, and all I could feel in that vacant space was the presence and force of my mother's love and my love for her.

That night when I drove home from the seminar, I felt different. I reflected upon my labyrinth of feelings while tears flowed down my cheeks interspersed with spontaneous laughter. Anyone looking into my vehicle observing this late night drama would have thought I was totally insane. Yet I felt ridiculously sane for the first time in a long time. Since my mom died when I was twenty-five years old, I decided to write her a letter. In the letter, I asked for her forgiveness for not recognizing how much she loved me. I declared how much I loved and missed her, and I forgave myself for holding onto a belief that did not serve me and hurt all the female relationships I had been in, starting with her. The letter was not long, but as I wrote, I continued to cry as the tears seem to cleanse my soul. I was not used to crying so deeply and spontaneously. Little did I know then that this was just the beginning of learning to cry and release my ongoing emotional pain.

My wife and I had still not shared with our family or our children the crisis we were going through. From my point of view, waiting left the hope of reconciliation. Later, I realized that she was attempting to move through this painful process systematically, waiting for the appropriate time. But the truth is that there is never a right time to share with your children that you are getting divorced.

Healing through the Fire

In her thoughtful books about dying and loss, Elisabeth Kubler-Ross outlined the stages of feelings that people must go through to ultimately heal and come to a peace within. We go through anger, sadness, loss, grief, and finally acceptance. Too often the silent ghost of denial can have us believe we have evolved through the fires of our pain, while in truth, we are still standing in the fire, pretending that we have walked across the hot coals. The challenge of denial is that it we are unaware of it while we are in it.

When Stuck—Do Something!

I needed a change. I needed to be revived. Like a galactic black hole, I felt everything collapsing inside in spite of my episodic revelations. Fortunately, in another seminar, I found out about an organization called Flying Doctors of America made up of professionals and lay people who want to bring health care to indigent countries. It was based in Atlanta, Georgia where I lived, and after a conversation with Alan Gathercoal, the President of the organization, I decided to go on a mission trip to Mexico that was leaving in a few weeks. He was as excited as I was, since they had never had a chiropractor participate on these mission trips before. The trip was extraordinary, yet the whole time I was gone, I thought about my family. There I was, far away, secluded high in the Sierra Madre Mountains, serving hundreds of thankful people in impoverished villages, thinking of my wife and children.

I had hoped that perhaps being away doing something so different might be the catalyst for my wife to realize that she did not want to end our relationship. As I was growing and discovering new things about myself, I continued to believe our relationship would prevail through those difficult times.

I was only gone one week, though it seemed like months. I envisioned going on future mission trips and saw the possibility of all health professionals working together to serve others. I got excited seeing the ways in which healthcare would be different if all professionals worked together in the states like we were in these remote villages. I also hoped that as differently as I felt about myself from this adventure that I would be greeted differently at home.

Chapter 2:
Waking From Denial

When I came home, I felt reborn, though the reception from my wife was guarded and distant. We hardly spoke and walked on eggshells around the house, keeping a lid on our feelings around the children. I went to work, came home, and continued to hope that somehow this marriage was not going to end. At night we slept in the same bed, silently drifting into sleep, turning away from each other. It felt like isolation separated us within the small space beneath our covers in the dark. In one sense, I was feeling better about myself. I was exploring and discovering new, creative talents and was growing emotionally and spiritually. Yet it was still pain and tears that echoed through my restless sleep and dreams.

After I'd been home for about a week, we went to see a movie. As we were driving home, I said something like, "So, where are you? What are you feeling?"

"I don't want to talk about it right now," she replied.

My hands tightened around the steering wheel. I'd been dreading this conversation but avoiding it was making me crazy inside. We had been living in silence, struggling inside with our own confusion, fear, and darkness. Since we couldn't speak about it in the house around our children, this seemed like the perfect time, so I continued to press. Even as I am writing this, I can still feel the helplessness of that moment. I felt possessed.

"Why don't you want to talk about this now?"

"I just don't want to talk about it," she said defensively.

I pressed more, "tell me something." "Anything."

Finally she shouted back, "I still want a divorce."

I don't know what I was expecting, but those words felt like a shotgun blast tearing open my face, hurling me out of my fantasies and denial. I had gone to seminars, workshops, and a mission trip, willing to do whatever it took to keep my family together, but it was not enough. It was simply too late. While I'd been struggling to find the magic key to keep us together, she'd been moving forward, envisioning her life without me as her husband. It seemed that nothing had changed for her since day one. I had lost her, and now it was final. I had failed her as a husband, I had failed my children, and I had failed myself. We drove up to our home, and she got out of the car. I sat there realizing that the time had come to face the most difficult moment in my life—sharing our planned separation and divorce with our children and family.

Hindsight

How do we get to this horrible place? It is certainly not our intention to eventually divorce when we first fall in love and decide to get married. Hopefully, we anticipate our marriage will last forever. Yet more marriages are failing, more divorces are occurring, and more children are being raised without the loving support of a mom and dad living together. How do we slowly slip out of love and fall from grace with our partner? My own experience tells me it is quite easy. It's as easy as accepting illness as a normal state of health as we age. It's as easy as a plant wilting and eventually dying when it is not nurtured. We enter into relationships thinking we already know what to do to manifest a wonderful, lifelong partnership. Yet who have been our role models for healthy, passionate, understanding relationships? Perhaps you have been fortunate to have witnessed a mom and dad display loving, respectful qualities your whole life. But for most of us, our idea of romance and partnering has come from television, movies, and the not-so-perfect role models within our communities. The truth is we have to learn how to cultivate a relationship and see it as a mirror of our own desire to evolve emotionally and spiritually. We have to learn to respect our partner even when we may be in disagreement or feeling stressed. We have to take the time to communicate with each other and learn to listen compassionately. We have to learn that it is all right to be angry sometimes, but that it is not all right to take that anger out on our partner in a mean-spirited way. We have to learn how to be tender even when we're fatigued. We have to learn how to forgive and understand that broken promises take time to heal. Marriage works when two people continually strive to grow together, share visions and dreams, and honor, respect, appreciate, and trust each other along the way.

Somewhere in my marriage, I began taking my partner for granted. I became judging rather than loving, critical rather than compassionate, demanding rather than appreciative. In the process, the light of love began to diminish until it was just an occasional flicker. It was understandable that my partner eventually wanted a divorce. She felt that I had probably wanted a divorce for years. And sadly during those times, I began liking myself less and less. The more we each felt judged, the more our affection diminished and the more I agonized within myself. To the outside world, our marriage looked stable and near perfect. We had become successful holistic chiropractors. We had a nice home. We had two beautiful, wonderful children. We had achieved goals that we had envisioned. We shared similar holistic values, spiritual ideas about evolving and learning, goals for our children, and close relationships with our families. And after being married for fifteen years, we were now faced with sharing our separation and pending divorce with them. There was no turning back, and as much as I tried to remain calm and focused, I was afraid and in agonizing pain.

When I reflect back upon all of this, I realize we tend to feel better when we feel another person's love and appreciation, yet truly we are best when we give our love and appreciation unconditionally. As I felt my love diminishing during the relationship, it felt like a slow burning disease was degenerating my core. As much as I wanted to heal the disease, I became another victim to it like so many others before me.

Sharing with the Ones You Love

How do you tell your family and your children that you are getting divorced? How do you spare them the pain and sorrow that they are going to feel? We are not responsible for other people's reactions, yet I knew I would feel like I was. I had been masterful at feeling guilty during this whole process and right then I was swimming in an ocean of fear and guilt.

In one instant, all relationships within the family become fragile and unpredictable when there is a divorce. It is important to understand that in most situations your families have not been prepared for what you are about to share with them. Their lives, in most instances, are about to dramatically change. The ripples of pain affect each person differently. Each friend and family member will have to walk through their own fire, experience their own reactions, and ultimately make their own decisions and choices. But there is one certainty—things will never be the same.

The Pain of Sharing with Others

My wife had shared with her family separately and privately. They lived in Atlanta. It was awkward each time I spoke on the phone with any of them. They never asked questions, and I never supplied answers as we gingerly avoided the subject. On the other hand, my family was coming to visit us during the beautiful season of spring in Georgia. Typically, my father came up from Florida in the spring, and my brother David and his wife Molly came down from Martha's Vineyard.

There are times when we resist sharing intimate aspects of our circumstances with the people closest to us. It's like jumping into the deep sea and exploring unchartered territory, feeling uncertain of the consequences and outcome.

When I finally told them, initially my family was in shock. My brother David and Molly tried to understand the problem. They had always had the ideal marriage in which mutual admiration and respect seemed to come easily for them. My father could not believe nor accept that we were going to get divorced. The more I tried to explain our difficulties, the more frustrating it became. My family that I love deeply wanted to fix the problem, whatever it was. I could feel everyone's tension: my wife's discomfort, my father's frustration, my brother and his wife's sadness, and my feelings of inadequacy. My father had lived long enough to see how divorce could cripple a family and the devastating affects it could have on the children. And these children were his grandchildren. My father, a businessman, knew how divorce could tear apart a family emotionally and ruin them financially.

I watched my father search for answers to keep my family together. He shared stories about couples he had known who ruined their lives because of a divorce. But sadly they fell upon deaf ears. I felt helpless. My family responded to this information like I had been responding for the past few months. What could they do or say to make us realize that we had to solve our problems and not desert them? And whatever those problems were, they were sure that they must be minuscule in comparison to the problems some partners have.

As much as they tried to help us, the frustration in the room thickened until finally my father echoed the words, "I do not want this divorce." As strong as my father's desire was to fix our relationship, it was not his to fix. My wife gathered her courage to voice these simple words. "It is not your life, and it is not your decision."

The Loss of Innocence

My son tended to be quiet, and shy, whereas my daughter was very expressive and communicative. These were my children, and I loved being a dad. I loved being involved in their lives, and as their dad who would have protected them from any danger, yet now I was the one delivering the sad news that would change their lives forever.

My children had grown accustomed to my elaborate stories, lectures, bedtime meditations, and prayers. One evening when my daughter could not fall asleep, she called me into her room.

"What's wrong sweetheart?" I asked.

She looked at me innocently and said, "I can't sleep daddy. Can you please give me a lecture?" That was one of the many precious, amusing moments of being a father.

She gently fell into a beautiful sleep as I kissed her forehead and said, "pleasant dreams." As I left the room, my heart was pounding with joy and love, but at this present moment, my heart was pounding for a different reason.

As Nathaniel and Julia sat on our bed, I thought of all the times we had shared stories and games as a family. Now the time had come to share with them what I had been dreading for so long. Was there any way to make it easier for them? What special words could I share so that they could understand the positive aspects of divorce? All I knew at the time was that I hated that moment more than anything. All my efforts to save our marriage from being torn apart had failed. How do you sugar coat to your children that their mom and dad are getting divorced? You can't. At some point the words come awkwardly from your lips, and then there is silence. Dead silence.

I do not remember much about that evening. I maintain a landscape of details with so many memories, yet the conversation, feelings, and facial expressions of that evening have been erased from my mind.

In their innocence and innate wisdom, I believe children are always being guided by an internal survival mechanism and that they are wise regardless of their age. They often teach adults more than we can ever teach them.

To my surprise, once my children digested the complex emotional turbulence that stormed into their world, they needed and wanted to know answers to the most basic, practical questions. I was living in some fantasy that they would scheme up various ways to get their mommy and daddy back together like in some old

Disney movie from my childhood. But they wanted to know how this separation was going to directly affect their lives. If I had been sad before, I was even sadder now. I needed some fantasy.

I cannot even imagine the feelings and thoughts my children were having, but the immediate necessities in their lives were tied to questions like:

- Does this mean we'll be moving? Where will we be moving?
- Do we have to change schools?
- Who will pick us up after to school and take us to dance and soccer practice?
- Who will we be living with?
- How will this affect us?

And even a humorous question like my son asking, "does this mean you won't be checking my homework every night?"

My children's concerns were very real and just as confusing to us as they were to them. We tried to reassure them that whatever happened, their mommy and daddy loved them both very much and that we would make sure all their needs were taken care of. I said repeatedly, "There is nothing more important to us than your happiness," though the words may have seemed meaningless to them in those moments.

Throughout this time, I still lived at home and slept in the same bed as my wife. But when we went to sleep, it felt as if we were separated by an ocean, knowing that the inevitable was getting closer. It was time for me to begin looking for a new place to live, both physically and emotionally. At least one question would be answered for my children rather quickly. They would be living with their mom, and I would no longer be at their bedside each night reading a story and kissing them good night.

Chapter 3:
Navigating the Battlefield

It was official. Our family, children, and friends all knew we were getting divorced. Neither of us had spoken to an attorney, but I found myself at bookstores, browsing through divorce books. At the time, all of them shared the same essence, how to survive divorce and protect yourself. The more I read, the more frustrated I became at the legal complexities, especially if there were children involved. No wonder attorneys became the voice for couples meandering through the difficult passages of their lives. And sadly, no wonder couples felt like they were traversing a battleground defending and protecting their legal rights. In the world we live in, divorce is typically not a pretty sight.

It can bring out the worst in people, turning civil, kind, honest human beings into ruthless, self-centered, distrusting humanoids. The whole purpose of an attorney in these situations is to make certain that you are not taken advantage of by your soon-to-be divorced partner. During these emotional times, it is easy for an attorney to exacerbate each person's worse fears, creating more hostility and further breakdown. Wars can easily begin in which children are held hostage and suffer the consequences. Only the attorney wins and escapes unharmed.

This was a crazy time. I knew I wouldn't do anything to hurt my soon-to-be ex, but it was like being pulled into an emotional tornado in which healthy survivors were few. Divorce strikes a chord with many people. Soon friends and family began to position themselves on the battleground. Like a human-sized chessboard, divorce began to feel like a game that could only have only one winner. Some friends aligned with my wife and others with me, while others tried to remain neutral, though everyone had an opinion, a strong opinion. Some people who had been through a divorce shared their experiences, which typically had horrible consequences. I imagined that the more stories like those that my wife heard; the greater the distance would be between us. I imagined that she was feeling anxious about her financial security and our children, and I believed that in her heart she wanted to be fair. But "fair" can be a monster that rears its ugly head during a divorce. What may appear to be fair and reasonable to one person may feel like a turbulent storm of unjust unreasonableness to the other. Things were difficult enough trying to maintain a center of emotional equilibrium. I was falling into the nebulous category of being just a "man," a stranger who needed to be observed with cautiousness and distrust. Sadly, I found myself slipping into the same dark alley, sensing how easy it was to lose myself and feel a heightened anxiety each step of the way.

In the midst of chaos, anger, and fear, I needed to continue healing myself and discover a vision for my future and my children. But at the time, that vision seemed fragmented, like looking into a broken kaleidoscope. The more I read about divorce and the more stories I heard, the worse I felt. I simply wanted to escape. My sense of purpose seemed drained. Everything in life I had worked toward now felt meaningless. I needed adventures to help me forget everything.

A friend who had traveled throughout the world shared with me about his journeys and experiences, and the more he did, the more I realized there was nothing keeping me here except my children. My marriage had failed, and my world was turned upside down, so even if it were for just a few months, maybe that would be the escape I needed. So I did it!

Escape

For a month I traveled through Africa. I had always dreamed of the adventures of a safari, and it was finally happening. I woke with the lions, communed with gorillas, and watched the elephants playfully bathe in muddied streams. Another month, I trekked through the mountains of India and shared meditations with other soul seekers. Then I flew to Spain and hitchhiked along the countryside and the Mediterranean. Then I scouted the medieval castles of Portugal. Eventually, I walked the streets of Italy and France and shared stories with new friends.

Yes, I had escaped. Yes, I had many adventures. Yes, it was a dream fulfilled. And yes, I almost forgot my pain and sadness. But there was one thing I could not forget that hounded my dreams and was reflected in the eyes of strangers and in the spirits of animals. As I gazed into the night sky at the ethereal passing clouds, I was constantly reminded of my children.

I wondered how they were doing, what they were thinking. Those months had been a time of discovering a new spark in my soul, yet each day had passed with them having experiences that I had simply missed. I wasn't there to assist in their decision-making, share in their celebrations, or love them through their difficulties. I missed being part of their everyday lives.

And as I sat there deep in thought, a light illuminated the passages of my mind, and I felt a soulful smile resonating in my spirit. I felt a deep breath lift me past my tension, filling me with purpose and vision. As real as those months of traveling and escaping had appeared, I thanked God that inside me I had not missed the precious rhythms of time with my children. Instead I awoke from my meditative dream, and looked forward to share in the stories, prayers, and complaints of the day, and feeling the simple wondrous blessing of being a dad, as painful as that was at this time.

Moving On—Moving Out

The time had finally come for me to move out. I had to move forward with my life even though I felt like I was dying. I felt unbearable sadness as I drove away to my new rented apartment. I imagined that this sadness would eventually subside, but it didn't. Soon I was driving back and forth from their home to my apartment on a weekly basis. Each time I dropped them off, I drove away with a stark emptiness. It felt unnatural for me to drive them back to a home where their father no longer lived.

Chapter 4:
$100,000 Plus

Now that I had moved out, the fire of our divorce negotiations was getting hotter. I asked my wife not to hire an attorney. I had spoken with several friends and colleagues who had been divorced, and the stories were horrific. The consensus was that the more money you had saved, the more the attorneys would make. One friend, who was an attorney, shared that his divorce cost him $150,000 in legal fees. He was certain that if he and his wife had simply continued to communicate and discover mutually amiable agreements, they could have saved that money. And he was an attorney! As I continued to read books about divorce, it was easy to see how attorneys' enflamed the war like a deadly, sophisticated chess match between two people rather than empowering healthy dialogue. Ultimately, the more money each person was trying to protect, the more complicated the divorce would become, and essentially, the more money the lawyer earned. I also read that there were mediating attorneys who could, in essence, represent both people. Conversations with my wife were like walking on a tightrope. Leaning too far to either side could aggravate circumstances. Thankfully, she cautiously agreed, and then with a thoughtful stare said, "Only if it's a woman."

Calm Inside the Storms

In my heart, I knew I would never hurt my wife. This was the woman I had been married to who was the mother of our beautiful children. Yet our relationship was spinning into a complex orbit. We were both in a state of

25

anxiety and confusion about our lives, not knowing where we were going.

Our conversations with each other were civil when discussing chores, details, and responsibilities relating to our children but got tense when speaking about legal issues, assets, dividing property, and savings. At those times, we were like porcupines trying hard not to expose our quills. Regardless of how I felt about my own integrity, it was clear from her actions and responses that she was trusting me less and less. And now that we were living apart and officially separated, I no longer had any influence, even if I imagined I had had some influence in the past. Other people's fears and true accounts of their divorces began playing a deeper role in her mistrust. I was no longer Marty. I had simply become the man she was divorcing. After all, during our marriage one of her biggest issues was that she felt controlled and intimidated. She was determined not to allow that to happen during her separation and divorce. I still seemed to have a vote, but my votes were not always officially counted.

Single Again

Even though my wife and I were still legally married, I was now feeling like a single man. When I moved out, we gave each other permission to date. Many of my friends wondered why we were not officially divorced yet, even though I knew the process we were going through was important for our individual health and the health of our children. I truly felt that the more we communicated with each other, the friendlier our divorce could be. Rather than quickly divorcing I believed that time was working in our favor. We were all, kids included, embarking on a journey that continued to manifest obstacles and new challenges. Each decision required thoughtfulness as to how it would affect everyone. Anger was the last thing I wanted to be manifesting when we spoke with an attorney.

As I sat on the futon on the floor in my apartment, staring out the window, I felt strange. I had not lived alone for many years. Even though all the apartments were connected, my conversations with the other tenants were limited to a brief hello. I don't know what I was expecting, maybe something like summer camp where we all had sleepovers.

As crazy as I was feeling inside, life was simple. My two-bedroom apartment was easily decorated: a chair in the corner, a picture on the wall, a plant by the window, a bookcase lining up my favorite books, and a dining table for my children, friends, and future guests to share food and conversation. It was cozy and comfortable. I felt like I was beginning to get my life back, or in truth that I was beginning my new life. My inner strength was returning.

Yet I also felt guilty when I was feeling good because I was not in my children's life everyday. This created more freedom in my life, but I felt bad knowing that my wife did not have the same freedom. Why did I feel so guilty? I didn't ask for the divorce. I didn't want to leave my home and family. If she had more responsibilities than I did, wasn't that her choice? I was the one ultimately rejected in the relationship. As much as I was trying to create a healing vision for my family, I was also simply learning to survive, mending my wounds, and allowing myself to feel okay again. The teacher at that time happened to be guilt.

I believe my wife and I were trying to do everything possible to proceed in an honorable way. We both wanted the best for our children and that remained the guiding light. I believed she appreciated that I made our children a top priority. Everyday I called in the evening after work, asking them, "How was your day? Do you have homework? How are you doing? I look forward to seeing you tomorrow."

At times my children would say, "Dad, we just talked to you yesterday."

"I know, but just know I will be speaking with you everyday," I would say. I needed to speak to them daily as much as they needed to know I was in their life everyday. I couldn't imagine a father wanting anything less than that. I was motivated by both fear and love. I was afraid I could lose my children in the turbulent roller coaster of emotions that can arise out of divorce. I didn't believe I would lose them physically, but I was afraid of losing their trust and love. While I suffered from being separated from my children each day, my wife suffered with the difficulties of acting as a single parent, confronting the responsibilities and tensions of everyday life. Under the circumstances, I observed my wife and felt fortunate that she had also made our children a priority and was devoted to their wellbeing and education. I believed she wanted me to be involved in our children's lives as much as possible, particularly when it made her life easier. She just no longer wanted to be married to me.

Breakdowns

Ironically, probably the most heated arguments I had with my wife came after either one of us had spoken to a friend or family member who was trying his or her best to give loving advice. Initially, it felt almost impossible not to be influenced by friends and family's fears, concerns, and opinions. Once everyone was clear we were heading toward divorce, the catch word became "protection." It didn't take much when I was feeling emotionally vulnerable to be pushed further over the edge, even when it was done with caring, loving, hands.

During this time, my dad and I represented two entirely different worlds. He was the businessman, pragmatist, and essentially, dad. In his own way, he tried to save our marriage, but now the time had come for him to protect his son. He had seen the casualties of divorce, and he wanted to make sure I didn't do anything foolish. He had always been a great dad, consistently involved in my life, and now was no exception. I was the dreamer, the healer, the one who usually did things differently from the norm. I knew that my wife and I would somehow discover a spiritual path that led to healing and a healthy divorce. Regardless of our breakdowns, and regardless of what I felt from day to day, I reminded myself to continue healing and thinking of our children. When I spoke of this to my father, I could tell the words sounded contradictory to him, as well as everyone else. My father continued to share all the stories of people he knew who had been divorced and the mistakes many of the men had made. He shared the importance of taking action steps immediately to protect myself. Everything he said could have been true, yet the timing and the tone of the conversations weren't helpful. I needed emotional support, words spoken from the heart addressing my pain and offering encouragement. This was another lesson of hopes and expectations not being fulfilled. I was still an emotional wreck, and I needed to hear, "How are you feeling? Can I assist you in some way?" But that was not my dad. The more he heard my idealistic approach, the more he felt the urgency to share horror stories of people he knew whose lives had been ruined because they did not handle their divorce with the proper business attitude. I am certain my father felt as frustrated as I did when we got off the phone with each other. He probably thought,

"My son is such a dreamer." Yet when I got off the phone, I could feel the pressure of anger and frustration building inside. It was not good to be around my wife after these conversations. If anything, it showed how easy it was to escalate anger and fears during these fragile moments. No wonder divorces become so ugly when skillful attorneys are hired to represent each person.

One particular occasion, we began arguing while discussing some aspects of our divorce. As the tension and anxiety mounted between us, we were standing face to face screaming at each other. I could feel her defiance as she felt she no longer had to back down from me. As the tension grew, I gently pushed her backward, not realizing there was a bicycle behind her. She accidentally fell over the bicycle. When she quickly got up, she stood in front of me again, even more defiant. "I am not afraid of you. I am not afraid of you," she persisted.

I felt like I had sunk to a new all time low. I couldn't believe who we were both being at that moment. I had never hit my wife or any other woman in any relationship, and I certainly didn't mean for her to fall over the bicycle, yet at that moment I could see how good people could lose it and then justify their abusive behaviors.

Even though I had never been physically abusive in our marriage, I knew she had felt emotionally abused. If anyone knows your Achilles' heel, it is your partner of several years. Emotional abuse may take the form of judgments, blame, indifference, withholding affection, or even manipulative silence. Whatever way the subtle abuse manages to express itself, the result is the same even if it was not intentional or done with malice. We can be left with broken wounded hearts that may not learn from the experiences, evolve, or heal.

I stood in silence observing us, like watching a horrible movie in which I was the main actor. The more I tried to get out, the more I felt like a moth in a spider's web being tangled deeper and deeper, being squeezed until all my breath was gone.

Decoding Conversations

Thankfully, a few days later I had a realization. I needed to create a decoding technique in my brain so that each time I spoke with family or friends, particularly my dad, my decoding device would allow me to hear clearly what people were sharing from their heart without taking on the fear. The next time I spoke with my dad, all I heard were the simple words, "I love you." It has been said that the longest journey in life is from one's head to one's heart. Previously when speaking with my dad, I could not hear his heart or my own. Now when my father said, "Have you spoken with an attorney? Have you looked into child support and alimony laws?" all I could hear was "I love you son. I am just worried about you, and I want to keep you from being hurt."

I never did tell my father about the decoder; it wasn't necessary. Our conversations became less stressful, and I was able to engage with him. I knew he felt different as well when I was no longer reacting in a defensive or distant behavior. I began to feel nurtured by his caring. I realized once again how expectations cause suffering in relationships, and as I let go of my expectations, I could feel my dad's love deeper and deeper. I knew the decoding mechanism was simply a tool that was necessary at the time so that I could feel anchored to my own spirit during these unpredictable storms.

The next time I saw my wife, we both apologized for our behaviors, yet we understood this was still the beginning of a long journey. The process of our divorce was slow, and our family and friends didn't always understand my approach. I prayed that it would eventually become clear to everyone, especially us. I felt like I was inventing the wheel blindfolded. When close friends inquired as to what was taking so long, I did not always have clear answers. It must have been going into the second year even though time seem like a blur from when my wife first asked for our divorce. I knew that some divorces occurred within a few months, and some perhaps a year, but I had no timeline other than feeling the pace of our own healing. After all we were writing our own script for our own family.

Chapter 5:

Elephant Man

After sixteen years of marriage, I was now a single man entering a new world that I was unfamiliar with. Who was I going to be as a single man? I was hurting and hungry for affection and passionate emotions. And I needed to have fun. But this road had many bumps and detours, especially in the beginning.

When I boldly shared my interest with the first woman I was truly attracted to, her words echoed through the canyons of my soul. "Thank you very much. I really like you, but not that way. Can't we just be friends?" She was concerned that I wasn't even divorced yet. Even though she was right, I felt emotionally divorced, and the "Can we just be friends?" felt like the kiss of death. Was this to be my destiny in relationships? Was it my fate to "just be friends" with the women with whom I wanted passion, intimacy, and love? I had avoided that as I was a younger, single man, but perhaps this was my karma for the future. I began to understand that the elephant on my back was invisible to me but quite noticeable to every woman to whom I was attracted. This elephant was burdened by confusion, sadness, frustration, and an unquenchable horniness. I had a desire to feel love, tenderness, caring, and touch again. At the same time, I felt weak and vulnerable, like I had lost my manhood. My wife had rejected me even after trying so hard to win her back, and now I was needing to invent a new future in the world of intimate relationships.

When I finally did enter an intimate relationship, I felt like I was eighteen years old again. I felt emotions I had not experienced in years. There was passion, fun, excitement, spontaneity, and dysfunction. Like a teenager, my emotions were a constant roller coaster of tremendous highs and crashing lows. During this period, I did not always recognize who I was—for better or for worse. During this time, I lied to my children for the first time. I felt awful. I told them I was attending a chiropractic seminar one particular weekend when that was the last thing on my mind. I certainly wasn't going to tell them the truth that their dad was developing an addiction for passionate intimacy. As much as I hated myself for lying to them, my dysfunctional thirst for emotional highs and lows were part of my survival at the time.

Mediators, Laws, and Fairness

As the months passed, my wife and I agreed on a mediator. He was an attorney we both knew who had been a patient in our office. We both liked and respected him, even though he was a man. He had been through a divorce, as well, and knew first hand how ugly, messy, and costly divorce could be. In retrospect, he wished he'd have been able to create a healthy divorce with his ex-wife. His children suffered the consequences of a painful divorce in which conflicts were never resolved.

There are many issues that are important to understand regarding mediators, attorneys, laws, child custody, child support, alimony, division of assets, unpaid debts, and the fairness of dividing savings. Each state has its own laws when it comes to all these concerns. It is important to do your homework. There are many books that cover this information in detail, and it is important to approach your divorce like you are dividing a business. My goal is to share with you the importance of approaching this situation with a kind, compassionate spirit, and a sincere desire to be fair while maintaining one's own integrity.

I remember sitting in the lawyer's office with my wife and attorney. I was feeling very uncomfortable, but trying hard to conceal my vulnerability. A mediator is part legal council and part therapist. A good mediator creates a context for a healthy divorce. He lays out a plan of action, like an architect drawing plans for a house. He becomes an ear to both people as they express their concerns and fears, and he attempts to build a bridge for constructive conversation. A mediator cannot do the work for you, nor should he. This is why you need to be in consistent communication with each other. Even arguments are better than not communicating at all. Communication creates the possibility for healing. But even when you are trying to discover well-intentioned solutions to perplexing obstacles, the floor can feel like it is falling out from beneath you in the process. The first meeting with the mediating attorney made me realize that we both had more work to do individually as well as together before our next meeting. We left frustrated, even though our attorney acknowledged our willingness to negotiate a fair divorce. It was hard to imagine what a divorce could turn into when two people did not care about being fair.

Respecting our Children

One weekend I was picking up my children to bring them to my apartment. They each had a miserable expression on their face. I asked them what the problem was. "Why do we have to go to your apartment today?" they asked. The question hit me straight and hard like a bullet. I was speechless for a few moments before pulling the car off to the side of the road. I realized they enjoyed sleeping in their own beds, surrounded by their games and friends in the comfort of their own neighborhood. Ultimately, I was left asking how and why did I let this happen to my children? They did not get to vote regarding the divorce, and now their life was compromised because of it. My guilt, sadness, and pain consumed my spirit at that moment.

As I turned toward my children, I answered their question the only way I could, with the truth. I told them that they were not wrong and that they did not do anything wrong. And most important they were not wrong for expressing what they were feeling. I was hurt, but I was responsible for the circumstances. "I am sorry," I said. "I am sorry for your lives being disrupted. I am sorry that so many things are changing in your lives because of your mom and dad getting divorced. I am sorry that I have to pick you up and take you away from your home and friends, but right now, this is the only time I get to be with you both." I said I was sorry so many times during these phases of our separation and divorce. We were all growing through this together, and hopefully we would discover healing during this difficult time.

Reflection

It has always seemed so horrible the way children suffer through their parent's divorce. Too often I have seen parents make their children wrong for expressing their thoughts and feelings during these chaotic times. It is as if the children's emotions do not count. Not only did the children not get to vote on their parent's separation, but they are also asked to go along with everything without questions. Too often separated couples are so busy and self-consumed with their own stresses that they fail to recognize what is occurring in their children's lives. This becomes an easy time for children to be pushed aside, as their mom and dad try to discover their own new life. Children can feel like excess luggage when they feel their mom and dad are not emotionally and physically available for them. Sometimes as parents we are so righteous about children honoring their mom and dad, that we forget as parents to honor our children, as well.

Chapter 6:

New Relationships and Difficult Times

Life was changing faster everyday. It was hard to believe I had been on two other mission trips, one in Peru, and the latest to the Dominican Republic. Two years had gone by meandering through this separation waiting for all the pieces to come together. My wife and I were in new relationships, and we were getting close to finalizing our divorce. She decided to move to a different community with a better school system for the children. We had lived in the country as a family but that no longer served its purpose. The children were isolated out there, especially without me being a part of their daily lives. My wife thought it best that they move to a neighborhood surrounded by other children, and under the circumstances, I agreed. It was also a way for her to move away from a home filled with painful memories and to further declare her independence.

The timing, though, could not have been worse for my daughter. For her it meant entering high school in a new location. Changes were difficult for her, and this meant she was not going to the same high school as her friends. She was angry that her parents separated. She was angry that she had to leave her friends, and she was anxious about starting a new school where she did not know anyone. After the first week in school, she had a sign above her bed that said, "I hate school." I felt my daughter's pain and tried to assist her as best I could.

This is such a delicate time in a teenager's life. As a loving parent you try to discover the clear answers to your children's problems, though it is not always easy. And when parents are divorced, it becomes that much more difficult. Parents are no longer on the same team, sharing the same vision. I could hear my daughter crying out for attention and love. Added to that, our children witnessed their mom and dad being in new relationships, which only complicated things for them. Thankfully, we consulted with a family therapist. This allowed our children to voice their feelings and thoughts, which helped in their recovery as best as it could at the time.

And most important, we created an option for our daughter. If she made good grades and decided after a semester that she still wanted to go to her original high school, we would make arrangements for her to do so. With this option, she truly felt like we were listening and paying attention to her, and it allowed her to make a choice. Inevitably when the time came, she indeed did make a wise choice, remaining in her new school.

Important Transitions

When mom or dad enters into new, intimate relationships, this is a crucial time in each family member's life because many worlds collide. For the child, mom or dad being with a new person can mean less time spent with the child. And if that new person is in the child's home, it can truly feel like an invasion. Typically, children have only seen their parents being affectionate with each other, and now there is someone else who is even sharing dinner with them!

Like many girls, my daughter expressed her feelings outwardly, and I knew how she felt emotionally at all times. She was having a difficult time with this other man in the house, feeling like her privacy had been somewhat invaded. The good news was she was old enough for me to talk with her about it. But like most boys, my son was less communicative, especially about his feelings. If I asked him how he was feeling his simple reply was, "Fine." I remember visiting when my ex-wife's new boyfriend was over. He was a nice guy, though initially, we were like planets trying not to collide when we were both in the house. My main concern was that he treated my children and my ex-wife respectfully, and thankfully he did. My son was still young at that time, and this new man was in his home more than I was. I worried that my son might be confused as to how to feel about him or about the role I was going to have in his life in the future.

My heart was heavy, and each time I drove off to my apartment I cried my way home. I knew that the only way to lessen my son's confusion was to demonstrate consistency and commitment to his daily life. I wanted to tell him that I would always be his dad, yet I knew that only by participating in his baseball, basketball, and schooling would he truly know in his heart that his dad was never going to leave him—and most important that he was only going to have one father.

Rage then Transformation

New intimate relationships that may promise a future can change how people behave and think. Feeling attractive to a new partner and feeling passion is like an addictive drug. For me, the more passion I felt, the more I wanted. Being married for years without that can be like living in a desert, thirsting for water. When we finally have someone appreciating us, finding us attractive, telling us how special we are, it can affect our choices, actions, and behaviors. My ex-wife and I were both being appreciated deeply by someone else at this time, so in one sense I shouldn't have been surprised when she called me with some startling news, but I was!

We started out speaking about the information we would need for our next visit to the attorney's office. It was a straightforward business conversation with guarded emotions. But then I heard something I had not heard before. It had to do with the possibility of moving—out west. "It might be good for the children. A change might be healthy for them." I knew her boyfriend had lived out west and had desired to move back that way, but I wasn't prepared for this. It hit me straight on, giving me immediate emotional whiplash. I lost it. I couldn't believe she would even think of it as a possibility, and especially thinking it might be good for our children. Maybe she was testing me to find out how I would respond. Even if she had felt my deep love for her disappear over the years, she knew the commitment and love I had for our children. She had never seen it waver. My rational brain collapsed into anger and fear, seeing the disastrous divorce battleground that I had been trying so hard to avoid. One shout led to another, and who knows what words were exchanged. It didn't matter. The phone on the other end slammed down while I held my receiver for minutes, paralyzed with pain, fear, and rage. I saw my life that I once imagined would be exciting, unique, and wonderful shattering like a mirror on the floor. It was quickly becoming a life I did not want to live—not without my children. I could not move as I searched for an answer in the maze of my speeding, crazy thoughts. All I could see was the battle over our children. I wasn't going to let my children move away. I would fight, I would do whatever it took, and in the end I would probably lose that war, and my children would be the innocent victims of a typical divorce in which parents fail to imagine how their impulsive actions might affect their children their entire lives. Traditionally, courts always favor mothers, especially if they are good mothers. I finally unleashed my rage and screamed, filling the room with pain and despair. I felt nauseous and wobbly kneed as I made my way to the bedroom.

How did my life become such a mess? I closed my eyes and drifted into a meditation, calling on God for help. "I don't know the answer. I need your guidance." I repeated it like a mantra. My intellect and wisdom could only take me so far. I felt like I was running on hot coals that were burning my feet, yet my brain was frozen. The stretches of fire seemed endless, but I was helpless.

I had asked for guidance before, but this time I was truly on my knees because I couldn't stand without shaking. I had always had a relationship with a higher power since I was a child. It came naturally to me. It didn't feel religious, just true. Sometimes God answered, and sometimes there was the understanding that God works in mysterious ways. But this time I heard an answer, and I didn't have to wait long. The answer was precise and clear with no room to misunderstand the message. *In your deepest rage and anger, you will discover deeper love, wisdom, and compassion, and when you do, you will want to share that healing gift with others. Ask and you shall receive, but be prepared for what you ask for,* flashed through my mind. A moment ago, I had been feeling the rage of a hurricane, but then I felt waves of peace flow through me as things became crystal clear. There was only one person I could change and that was myself. I didn't know what the future would hold, but at that instant, I knew I was going to bring compassion, love, forgiveness, and peace to my family. I walked out of the bedroom, picked up the phone, and called my wife back. I simply apologized for anything I said that was offensive. I kept it short and simple and didn't explain about my experience or transformation.

My words, deeds, and actions began to carve a new path that made all the difference.

Reflections

I have often shared this story with others. Be willing to ask for guidance and listen to your own sacred place with the humbleness and openness that is necessary to truly hear. Each of us has the ability to go within and bring to consciousness the innate wisdom that is inherent in each of us. It is the willingness to trust that voice as a divine light that can lead us from our own despair. I believe when you hear that voice it will only lead you to healing and compassion and guide you toward actions that fulfill your heartfelt desires. The obstacles will still be there, but your vision will be clear as you move forward.

Chapter 7:

Mending Fences and Building Trust

After that day, things continued to change. I had surrendered my anger, some of my sadness, and most of all my fight. Over time, our partnership toward our children became the guiding light. On my wife's part, there was no further talk of moving, and I certainly never brought it up. Though I had no control over my wife's actions or thoughts, it was obvious that my transformation began to create an atmosphere conducive to a more civil and healthy divorce. I could feel her heart opening and she began trusting my behaviors more. This was slow, but it was a process with a committed vision. I never wanted my children to say to their dad, "Why weren't you there for us?" I showed up at my children's house more often when their mom was at work to make dinner, connect, and check homework. At the time my daughter was now well into high school, while my son was in junior high. I believe it was greatly appreciated by my wife for it made her life easier, and our children benefited from their mom and dad getting along better. It also began teaching them the value of healing and changing in healthy ways. Their family was not going about divorce in the usual way. At times that may have felt awkward to them as things can be for teenagers attempting to fit in with their peers.

One afternoon I was at their home, and I heard one of my daughter's friends say to her, "I thought your parents were separated or divorced." My daughter replied, "They are. They're just weird. They're both chiropractors." Though I understood the pressure all children might feel to explain the actions of their parents,

I knew this was an important conversation to have with my children. Indeed my children were destined to have "weird parents" in comparison to their friends. Sometimes it was weird food they brought to school for lunch, like fresh fruit and fresh vegetables. They didn't drink kool aid as children nor was coca cola and junk food kept in their home. And most of their friends had never even heard of an avocado, and of course had no desire to eat one when I offered them an avocado and cheese sandwich. Their birthday cakes were usually carrot cakes, quite delicious but weird, and at ball games their dad would be doing some chi gong exercises rather than just sitting for two hours on hard wood bleachers, or chairs. But my children's fate was delivered right from the beginning. They both were not born like most kids they knew in a hospital, they were born at home, a natural child birth with a mid wife without any drug intervention. They were not on medication like most of their friends for allergies and asthma, instead were receiving chiropractic adjustments, receiving herbs, and homeopathic remedies, and taught about the virtues of healthy eating, and nutrition. Even on holidays my children needed to explain to their friends why they celebrated both Christmas and Hanukah, since their mom was raised Christian and their father was raised Jewish. So from the beginning being raised in a southern town outside of Atlanta, Georgia, my children felt some pressure to explain their lifestyle to their friends. So it was not unusual where once again even in divorce their parents were "just weird."

And indeed, we were looking different than most separated and divorced families. I went to every one of my daughter's dance recitals and plays and every one of my son's basketball and baseball games. Sadly, I rarely saw other divorced fathers taking part in their children's everyday lives.

A few days later my children and I spoke about their mom and dad's separation and how it was different than some of their friends who had divorced parents. They shared how some of their friends hardly saw their dad, while others would spend every other weekend at their dad's house. As my children shared this with me I listened as they also said that their friends wished their situation was more like the circumstances they observed at their home. In essence even though my son and daughter may have thought their parents were weird, in their heart they were both glad we were weird in this way. They were glad that their mom and dad were becoming better friends, which allowed me to spend more time with them and more time in their home.

Remember, children never choose divorce or the difficulties their parents go through, and they are realistic and practical. They have so much happening in their world each day. My children were definitely happier and life was becoming easier for them as their parents were healing. Our healing made their healing easier.

Making it Legal

When the divorce became official, it simply felt like another day. For me, the process of healing, growing, and learning were the landmarks of this spiritually challenging journey. Making it legal was just a blip on the screen. In my heart, we had been divorced for several years. Instead of being a married couple with children we had become parents committed to their children, teaching them how to heal during difficult times. As we grew closer, sharing and being together even during holidays became normal and natural for us.

My family and friends were witness to the healthy divorce we had created. My father was not accustomed to people getting divorced and remaining friends. I can still remember him saying, "You're really different." He observed his grandchildren reaping the rewards from parents who were divorced yet who still cared about each other and shared mutual visions for their children. I cherish in my heart those simple words, "You are really different." It was hard to imagine people choosing to take the typical road of divorce once they understood the emotional cost of ongoing bitterness and the possible financial ruin, especially to hardworking families. During the years of separation and divorce, I have always been thankful that we made our children a priority, even during the most difficult times. I have always been blessed that my ex-wife is the mother of our children.

Chapter 8:

New Beginnings

The relationship with my ex-wife and our children continued to get better as the years went by. Like in any family or relationship, there were difficult times but that was part of the journey. We had made it and that felt great. We were still a family, even though we were divorced. In a sense our children had the best of both of us. I believe I became a better dad through the whole process of separation and divorce. Each moment felt even more precious and significant. Amazingly, my daughter was now a college student in Boone, North Carolina, and my son was deep in high school.

During these healing years I was feeling better and better about myself. I felt creative and passionate about life and even began writing about the healing journey of this divorce. Many of my friends coaxed me on, reminding me of how powerful a story it was and how it could help many people in similar circumstances who were battling through their separation or divorce. But the words were coming slowly, almost as if the written story was not ready to be birthed. Maybe it just wasn't meant to be written. The more I tried to push the words out, the more the story resisted being told. I had written songs and poetry for many years so I understood the creative process.

One evening, my inner voice woke me in the middle of the night and said, "Put aside the divorce book right now. I have another book for you to write, and it's going to be fun." Then the voice gave me the title *If Relationships Were Like Sports, Men Would At Least Know the Score.* I had been in few relationships during my separation and divorce, and with each person, I learned more about myself and began experiencing deeper levels of emotional and sexual intimacy. This was an area where my ex-wife and I had struggled. Rather than being joyful and fun, sex had become calculated and unfulfilling. But this was something I had wrestled with long before I got married. I was simply too much in my head when it came to sex rather than being present emotionally and enjoying the moment.

The next morning I began writing, and within three months I had a manuscript in my hands. It poured out of me, and it was fun! As I wrote about relationships, it became clearer to me why some relationships improve while others dissolve like a sand castle. During this fruitful time, I continued to hear that mantra inside, "As you continue to heal, you will share this healing with others." What occurred in the near future was unpredictable and unexpected. At times it can be unclear where fate, destiny, and free will shake hands with each other.

Ironically, as our healing evolved, my ex-wife and I discovered the qualities we enjoyed and appreciated about each other. We both were committed to our children, we shared similar professions, we enjoyed healthy lifestyles, and similar spiritual beliefs. If we had been on a first date with one another, we probably would have been impressed with how many things we had in common, a good beginning for any new relationship.

We had both been in romantic, intimate relationships and were discovering things about us in the process. Though it wasn't planned, subtle feelings of connection began to spark within us. The more we healed, the more our friendship developed. This allowed me to spend even more time with our children and inevitably my ex-wife.

Magic

It started innocently enough. We were taking my son to a friend's house to spend the night. "Would you like to go for dinner?" I asked. I had no idea how that one sentence would change my life. Dinner led to a movie. It was Saturday night, and neither of us were in a relationship with anyone else. How does one stop what feels like fate? We welcomed the evening cautiously, and the first rays of morning light seemed to be witness to a miracle as we held each other in a joyful embrace.

It truly felt like an invisible force that brought us back together. It had a magical quality to it like a Disney Movie with a miraculous ending. Just like I had not consciously planned for our divorce, I also had not consciously planned for us to reconnect and marry again nine months later. Yes, marry! I believed deeply that we had consciously changed and realized our life worked better for our children and each other when we were together. Initially, our future showed great promise. We were already friends, we had walked through many fires, and financially our life became more fruitful and abundant. It was not perfect, but we had both discovered that the relationships we had with others were not perfect either.

Everyone was happy for us, and though I anticipated our children responding joyously, they were intuitively cautious and uncertain. After all, they had the best of both of us just the way it was. Now they were being asked to take another walk through the fire with their mom and dad. I truly believed it was all going to be wonderful, and I was committed to work on our relationship as much as I worked on our separation.

Our wedding was simple and beautiful as if from a romantic novel. It was at the home of my brother and his wife on Martha's Vineyard. My family was there, and my children shared how they had grown through the process of this divorce observing how their parents' friendship and love had added to the quality of their lives. They both had witnessed other families in which divorce tore the family apart. I was very proud of them as they shared from their hearts. It was an amazing day. I felt reborn and felt that life could only move forward with abundance and bliss. In some unexpected way, I felt I had been given a blessed gift. My family was together once again.

I could feel the new me in our relationship. I was more compassionate and understanding and more of a team player. I also felt that my ex, now my wife was earnestly changing, and our relationship had the promise of fulfilling new visions.

My friend Michael told me that I needed to write my story and begin leading healing workshops again. "This is a story people need to hear, and they need to hear it from you," he said. How many families have been poisoned by the magnitude of divorce? How many people have suffered from the results of broken relationships and simply learned to survive rather than truly heal. How many families have seen their bank accounts diminish from attorney fees, not realizing the high cost of anger, fear, and revenge?

Yes, I agreed, this was a story people needed to hear and to learn from. Yet each time I attempted to write it, the words struggled resisting the creative process, perhaps knowing the story wasn't finished.

Chapter 9:
The Body Speaks

When the body speaks, it is important to listen. Something may be spinning out of control even before we realize it. This is often when our bodies try to get our attention. It started with a chronic cough from a bronchial cold that would not disappear. Then one morning I woke up with neck and shoulder pain exacerbated by numbness and tingling radiating down my arm. I was extremely perplexed when a few chiropractic adjustments and massages did not alleviate the problem. The problem got worse, my energy was waning, and nothing I was doing was reversing the problem. I was like a typical patient who was hurting and did not understand the cause of the problem. I had an MRI of my neck, thinking that maybe I had developed a herniated disc. When it did not reveal a herniated disc, I was relieved but still in tremendous pain as I continued working. I couldn't move my neck or raise my right arm without pain and numbness radiating down to my hands. When I asked the doctor why I was having these severe symptoms when there was no evidence of a herniated disc, he said that there were significant small spurs pushing into the spinal canal and that that could be worse! I asked what was done for this condition, and he said cortisone and neck surgery.

My bronchial cough and shortness of breath also got worse. I felt like my body was deteriorating, so for the first time in thirty years, I visited a medical specialist. Thankfully, all the tests came back negative. No infectious disease was manifesting, yet my body was becoming weaker as the pain and cough continued, leaving me feeling powerless, emotionally and physically.

Finally, I spoke with a psychic to discover the underlying cause of these problems. This was not my usual approach to health conditions, yet the way in which it occurred could not help but get my attention. I was vacationing with my family visiting my father in southern Florida. Sitting in the sun, I felt older than the people who lived there. Typically, I would have been playing tennis and outdoor racquetball everyday. Now, I felt disabled and unable to participate in any physical activity. Even swimming was painful to my neck and shoulder. My niece had been visiting there, too, and when she went home to New York, she saw her psychic and told him about her family. The psychic stopped her when she mentioned her uncle. "Something is going on with him deep inside," he said. When my niece shared this with me, I asked her if she had said anything to him about me. Nothing, she said. This immediately sparked my curiosity.

I often share with my patients that even when you think you are sensitive to your body, many blind spots remain. These are things about ourselves we can't see or don't want to see. I called the psychic, and we agreed to a phone session. As the session progressed, many of the emotions I was feeling but not wanting to feel about my second marriage emerged. It had been less than two years since I said, "Would you like to go out for dinner?" and now unhealthy communication patterns from our first marriage were developing again. Even though I was trying so hard to make this relationship work, it was dying. As the relationship was falling apart, my body was responding like a mirror image by getting sicker and sicker. As the session with the psychic continued, I realized the depth of sadness and anger that was being suppressed in my body. It was devouring me from the inside out. When the session was over, I had the gut wrenching feeling that our second marriage would be over soon as well.

Oh, how I wish I had a better story to share with you. As I tried to create a healthy dialogue with my wife, the frustration grew, and sadly our communication become more and more infrequent. It was deeply disturbing to me that I was now coaching others to increase intimacy and passion in their relationships yet felt helpless in my own. During one particular argument, knowing the end was near, I shouted, "I want a divorce." I wanted to be the first to say it this time, but I was also hoping for a different response, some resistance, an expression of shock, a good fight from the other side. But there wasn't any. In a moment of anger and frustration, words had come out of my mouth, and the offer was accepted without hesitation! Not so much in the words she spoke, but in the words that were never spoken.

When it finally sunk in, I was devastated. Once again, I asked myself how this happened. For a brief moment, there was the possibility of joy and abundance in our new marriage. We had visited our daughter in Spain who was studying abroad. We were together once again as a family. There was less financial stress, and hope that our relationship would evolve in healthy, passionate ways and that there would be many more trips together as a family in the future. But now it seemed that was not to be part of our destiny.

As the reality became clearer, I became angrier. I thought I had truly changed. Even friends and relatives had noticed the difference. I never even imagined the possibility of a second divorce, and definitely not from my first wife. It seemed impossible!

Even as I am writing this, it is hard to believe that this is my story, my life. It was like a recurring nightmare. Why was I having such horrible dreams?

Deja-vu

Once again I was faced with anxiety, fear, and rage along with wondering how to share this with our family. Initially, I wrote a letter to my father and brother explaining the circumstances and my feelings because I did not have it in me at the time to answer questions on the phone. My body and spirit felt frozen in anger and disbelief. What do you say when people ask those questions like, "What happened?" I simply had a feeling in my gut and wanted to throw up. No explanations could justify it or bring clarity to the situation. I was standing in the fire wanting to run, but it seemed to stretch into the distance for eternity.

The look on my children's face said it all. They were now grown ups. We all felt the energy in the room shift when my wife and I said we needed to tell them something. Even though I was the one who uttered the words divorce this time, I wanted to fight for our relationship and at least see a marriage counselor to discover what subtle forces were working to disintegrate our marriage. That never occurred. In retrospect, I would recommend that to everyone.

I let my wife tell our children the inevitable. She was resentful and angry that I had handed her the gun to shoot those damaging words that would tear at our children's hearts. "Your father and I have decided to get divorced. We tried, but it has just not worked." I knew my wife was painted as the villain. I understood but wanted no part of it, even though I was an equal in our partnership. Though I sat silently, I was not an innocent bystander. I was guilty of the same crime; I just didn't fire the gun.

That was the most horrible night of my life. It felt like telling my children that both their parents had died. Their faces filled with shock, loss, and anger. "Why did you get remarried?" they screamed. "Why did you get back together? Why, why, why?" After their abrupt storm of rage and pain, there were no other words to speak. A silent, penetrating darkness engulfed any light that remained. My children went upstairs, and my wife proceeded to our bedroom. I sat motionless for a while then went upstairs where both my children were huddled together, lying in bed. As I climbed into bed with them, I snuggled them close, as we all continued to cry. I remember saying, "We will get through this. We will get through this," trying to comfort them. We remained like that for what seemed hours.

In a different circumstance I may have never gotten legally married again. It had become obvious in my life at least, that it wasn't pieces of legal paper that held relationships together, but it was the choices that people make to share their love openly and honestly and continue each day to be with one another. But, when you remarry your own partner it is different, especially if you share children together. The very thought bringing one's family back together and making life easier for everyone, financially and emotionally can be an attraction that is difficult to resist. I did not like to think of myself as naïve, but I was! I entered in this second marriage, totally oblivious to the possibility that it could end. It wasn't possible that we would actually remarry only to divorce again. I never even considered it, and it was not on my radar screen. I entered this marriage with the innocence of a school boy, turning over my heart and bank account. I wasn't wrong doing that, I was simply foolish. I would have been different if I had married someone else. I would have been less naïve. I would have realized that two people can indeed choose different roads and fall out of love. There is nothing like feeling anchored down with anger, and feeling the loathing of one's own poor judgment. Now I felt all that anger, and how I was ultimately responsible for my children's emotional struggle and their pain.

Chapter 10:
Legal Ammunition

"Get out of my bed. I want you out of my room," my wife said as I was sitting up, reading against a pillow. She had chosen to sleep in a different room after we shared our pending divorce with our children, and now, I imagined, she was reclaiming her room by requesting I move out immediately. The words hit me like knives, yet I met them with a tone of indifference as I declined her invitation. It was evident that the very words she was using were clearly declaring the boundaries of ownership. What moments before had been "ours" was being redefined. This was now *her* bed, her home, her house. Naturally, she grew angrier and more defiant. The more hostile she became, the more I resisted. I told her that it was fine if she wanted to sleep in her bed but that I wasn't moving.

I have read about intelligent, professional, evolved, people who commit horrible crimes in a moment of rage. I always found it hard to imagine how good people could fall into the darkness of temporary insanity. I was being tempted to that edge.

"I want you out of my room," I heard again as she raised a pillow and hit me. I did not like being hit, and I was still recovering from a neck injury, but I remained stoic, unflinching, in a way that just put acid on her wounds, irritating her further. She hit me again. Yes, it was just a pillow, but behind it was anger and resentment, making each blow feel like a ton of bricks. After the second strike, I looked her deeply in the eyes, and said, "Do not hit me again," clear as a laser beam more with purposeful intent than anger.

Thankfully, she did not and left to go to sleep in the other room. I do not know what might have occurred had she hit me again. But at that moment, I could see clearly how loving people could fall from grace and become a headline in the paper. This incident still gives me the chills when I think about. The next night, I slept in another room, which I continued to do until I found a new place to live.

Attorney Notice

A month or so went by, and we continued to decline though we were still living together. Just when I thought things couldn't get more devastating, something unexpected occurred. My wife casually mentioned she had spoken with an attorney, and handed me an official looking manila envelope. I was speechless, feeling as if I was in the eye of a tornado. Holding that manila envelope was like holding a serpent by the tail that was ready to quickly curl around and strike. Hours later when I was finally able to talk myself into opening it, my greatest fear was realized. It was indeed from—my wife's attorney! The pages shook between my fingers as I read the words coded in the cold, steel language of legalese. Everything we had avoided doing in the first divorce now seemed inevitable. My soul was screaming, but no sounds came out of my mouth.

As I reread the paragraphs dozens of times, hoping perhaps that I was wrong, the language of the letter was clear. But I was not wrong. It was a declaration of war. And in no uncertain terms it held me financially responsible for all the costs in this escalating battle.

Thankfully, my daughter was away at college, but my son was still a minor, attending high school and living at home. I was still living upstairs in a room next to my son's and using a realtor to help me find something suitable I could call home. This separation and divorce was different from the first one. It was over, we were over, and I needed to move forward as quickly as possible.

But when I got that notice from her attorney, I felt betrayed, deceived, and manipulated. Once again, we were walking through scorching fires, trying to find the healing lesson. At that moment, I was just trying to survive before being overtaken by the flames.

When I approached her regarding this, she said she did not realize what the document contained. "That's not the point," I said. "I can't believe that all this time you've been seeking council with an attorney." Regardless of what I said, my words were insignificant at this time. She felt that she had no choice. She was frightened and felt the need to protect herself, even more this time. Considering we were not speaking to each other except for icy stares and murderous smiles, this was the best communication we were going to have at that time. Whatever her reasons were, I felt like she'd taken off the gloves and hit me below the belt. The battle was just beginning, and I believed I had no choice but to protect myself, too, with the best divorce attorney I could find.

Attorney Game

I took the elevator up into the high rise office building. Marble floors, antique, exquisite furniture, and large glass windows framed the Atlanta skyline. I had been recommended to the best divorce attorney, and people like me were paying for these beautiful panoramic views.

As we sat and exchanged formalities, I shared my logical, rational story about why I felt victimized in this second marriage. He listened attentively, nodding occasionally, even said he knew the other attorney, and then proceeded to say something that straightened my spine. "I understand your feelings and legitimate claims, but none of that will truly matter. The laws are very specific and precise, especially relating to divorce."

To me my story was everything. Feeling betrayed *was* my legal case. Without my story, I felt hopeless and naked in this procedure.

In the meantime, I had to fill out endless forms disclosing my assets, savings, and business accounts, a simple fact-finding routine for any attorney. Ultimately, these forms represented how much I was worth, how much I was protecting, and how much money they could make by helping me protect everything I had.

After spilling my heart out over his mahogany table, he shared that his fees were $350 an hour and that he typically received a $5,000 retainer to open the case. I managed to talk him down to a $3,500 retainer and felt a little victorious, but as I left the building, I realized my victory was an illusion. I still felt nauseated.

This is what I call the attorney shell game. Everyone running the game knows what's going on except the person investing the money. The briefings from my wife's attorney implied that I would be responsible for all of my wife's attorney fees. It was that clause that sparked my anger and scared me into immediately seeking legal council. I was relieved when my attorney told me that this was just a legal formality and that I did not have to worry about it. He also said not to discuss anything with my wife other than the normal activities regarding our children from that moment forward. He would be communicating on a regular basis with her attorney and handle everything.

When I got home, it hit me like a baseball bat across my face. One person seeks out an attorney, that attorney sends an alarming letter to the other person in the relationship, which sparks that person to seek out his or her own attorney. Initially, each person breathes easier, believing this will provide protection. But then the realization hits: $350 + $350 = $700 an hour!

It seemed like only moments ago that my wife and I were on the same team, sharing dreams, and now we were paying $700 an hour to dissolve that team. So every time one attorney called the other or wrote a letter, the other attorney billed one of us in order to respond. In essence, as a divorcing couple, we were being charged twice. It is a master shell game. The attorneys need the divorcing couple to remain distant and angry with each other in order to escalate their bills. The last thing they want is for the two people to actually communicate.

Oh, don't we love to hear those words, "Don't worry, and just follow the recommendations?" Most of us can easily sell our soul during times of fear and pain if the promise of comfort and relief is offered in return.

Within two weeks, I received my first bill. It was $1,500 for a few letters, phone calls, and basic set-up costs. My attorney already had $1,500 in the blink of an eye, and the battle hadn't even begun. I was petrified. The word bankrupt kept going through my mind—we'd both be bankrupt, and our children would suffer the consequences. I agonized over what to do.

Divorcing My Divorce Attorney

As crazy as it seemed, not that long ago I had been teaching couples the importance of communication and healing, and to avoid attorneys during divorce. Those profound lessons about compassion and forgiveness seemed to be from another lifetime. I wanted to sign up for my own seminar, but the workshop leader wasn't available.

Now I was faced with another dilemma. How do I divorce my attorney? It sounded funny when I thought about it and shared it with friends, yet I felt more frightened by my attorney's fees and the consequences of following his recommendations than my wife. Everyday we continued our non-communication, money was being drained from our bank accounts, money that we had saved for years.

I called a friend who was an attorney and asked him how to legally divorce my attorney. He understood because he had been through a divorce and experienced the financial and emotional stress on his own family. His advised me simply to write a letter of dismissal and to carefully read the contract I had signed, especially in reference to the retainer.

Before I wrote the letter, I approached my wife and shared my anxieties with her. I sincerely let her know my concern about us becoming bankrupt if we did not begin communicating. I recommended that we seek out a therapist who could assist us through our divorce. She was unwilling to dismiss her attorney, yet she was agreeable to the idea of divorce counseling. I had just broken attorney rule number one; I was communicating with my wife. As brief as it was, I felt a tinge of hope, very slight, but something.

During this time, I actually broke one of my own rules. I was in my car, speaking to my daughter on the phone. It was not a good time to talk with her, but she had called from college, so I answered. Anger and fear were pounding through my veins as I shared with her why I was so upset. My daughter had become a wonderfully compassionate listener who also could bring much wisdom to any conversation. But I had never spoken negatively about her mom before. Throughout the first divorce, I had never used our disagreements to manipulate my children until this moment. When I got off the phone with my daughter, I did not like how I felt. I could taste the poison in my mouth. I never wanted my anger to overflow into my children regarding their mom. She was still a great mother. I called my daughter back and apologized. "Dad you don't need to apologize. You are upset. I understand," she said.

"Thank you for being such a beautiful, understanding loving daughter, but I will not share my anger about your mom with you again, or with Nathaniel," I said. And I believe I have not!

As parents, one of the worst things we can do is to say mean things to our children about the other parent. We must remember that the relationship between children and their parents is sacred and eternal.

Clearly, relations between my wife and I spiraled down quickly once attorneys got involved. This took our fears and defensiveness to a whole new level. We liked to think of ourselves as good people, nice people, but before we knew it, we were both saying and doing things we could never have imagined. Being desperate to stop the spiral and not go bankrupt, I had to divorce my divorce attorney. I knew that would be healthy and positive, but it wasn't enough. What we really needed was to learn how to communicate again, even when it was really painful.

Chapter 11:
Shifting Relationships

There are many stages in the process of healing, though the first is often motivated by the instinct to survive. We become so entrenched in the battle that we don't notice the dead bodies stacking up along the way. Even though I was still angry and distrusting of my wife, I was motivated by fear to shift directions and discover new possibilities. I often hear people comment that it is difficult for them to imagine being friends with their ex-spouses and forgiving them. At that time, I could not imagine it either.

One day I called my wife's attorney requesting something, and soon after my attorney called me sounding quite upset that I had called my wife's attorney. I could only imagine that her attorney had called him and mentioned my call. To both attorneys, I must have seemed like a radical, misbehaving client. I was breaking all the rules, maybe even spoiling the whole divorce game. He said it was his job to communicate with the opposing attorney's office, and it was best if I did not interfere with that process. Of course, this created the perfect time to politely share with him that I had sent him a letter, asking for a divorce. I told him that we were going to seek divorce therapy and thanked him for his help. I know I caught him off guard as he shared the danger of this decision, but, ultimately, he wished me well.

At that moment I knew I made the absolute right decision, yet everything else remained the same. Confusion, anger, and fear were my constant companions. And now I was without legal council and representation while my wife still had her attorney.

A lot of people probably thought I was out on a limb whereas I figured I'd just cut down the trunk of the tree. I put my faith in following the healing work I had taught others, and prayed that I knew what I was teaching.

The first step was to be willing to receive healing and healthy guidance and practice compassionate listening. The message I had received from the first divorce was still profound and clear. In my darkest rage and anger, I would discover greater love, compassion, and forgiveness. The ultimate storm was still on the horizon, though, because I was not yet experiencing compassion and forgiveness. I was not even close.

In fact, I was up to my neck in protection and survival. I was becoming a person I didn't know, someone whose path had changed along the way. If getting divorced the first time was shocking, divorcing for the second time from the same person felt frightening and surreal, like an episode of the Twilight Zone. It was not the life I had signed up for. Though I knew I would never commit suicide, thoughts of suicide meandered through my mind. I began to understand how our thoughts could create a canvas of hopelessness and struggle in which taking one's own life could seem like a noble act. I had a friend years ago who did commit suicide when he was going through a divorce with his wife. Sadly, none of his friends knew how deeply he was suffering. He seemed to have it all on the outside. Even though he was a successful chiropractor, intelligent, funny, easy to be with and easy to talk to, something brought him to a dark place where suicide seemed like the only answer. I cried for hours when I heard the news. Only a month before I had sat next to him during a seminar, and he never mentioned a word of his difficulty

DIVORCE: AN UNCOMMON LOVE STORY

at home or at work. He just was his usual charming self. I never wanted to let my mind slip that deeply into despair, and thankfully I had wonderful children, family, and friends that gave me powerful reasons to continue to live and ultimately grow in healthy ways from this experience.

Therapy Sessions

Within a few weeks, my wife had found us a therapist. Initially, I felt as if the therapist was a referee in a gladiator fight to the death. Considering that we had not spoken in a couple of months, it felt uncomfortable facing each other in his office. I wasn't certain what was going to occur during these sessions, but I knew I wanted to create healthy resolutions between us quickly as possible. The longer our divorce continued, the more it cost, the more we suffered, and the more our children and families were affected by the toxic relationship. But this road was just beginning, and it had many bumps, twists, dips, and detours.

These sessions were not simple. Honestly, they were intense, at times hostile, and often evoked feelings of hopelessness. But even at its worst, I reminded myself that it was better than not speaking.

Inner Healing

I have found that regardless of what is going on, it is essential to discover a healing journey within. Thankfully, I am someone who lives a healthy lifestyle and teaches it to my patients each day. Taking care of and serving others has always been a gift for my own ongoing healing process. Eating healthfully, exercising, and meditating have all been paramount in my wellness, and most important, receiving healing work through chiropractic and other holistic modalities that align my body, mind, and spirit. But, it was the healing gift of music that nurtured my soul in the evening hours before going to bed by playing my guitar and singing my own songs. I had been a song writer since I was nineteen, and now singing and writing became my dear friends that guided me into a peaceful sleep.

During this time I also reconnected with an old friend who is a fantastic musician with a music studio in his home. After a brief conversation, he invited me over to reminisce, have fun, and record one of my songs. I felt like a kid in a candy shop. I was in heaven! I had always wanted to see how my songs could sound with some professional arrangements and backup. At the time, I could not conceive of the magic awaiting me. I simply knew I was having fun and feeling creative. This was a welcome break from the struggles my wife and I were facing in therapy.

Hostile Strangers

Our therapist attempted to assist us in a healthy dialogue. "Are you both certain you want a divorce?" The word yes seemed to echo through the room. "Well, then, who wants to start?" he said. I remember feeling that I never wanted to be friends with my wife again. As a cloud of resentment and distrust filled the room, it was difficult to believe that healing could happen, but deep inside I trusted the path of healing through healthy communication. At that moment, though, it was frozen deep inside, waiting to be thawed. In the meantime, we held our positions strategically as if on a battlefield as hostility and fear sprayed like machine gun bullets.

Our therapist was an older, gentle, wise man, and I prayed he was up to the task of assisting us through these difficult times without getting seriously wounded in the process. After all, it is the therapist's goal to maintain an impartial, safe space for each person so that neither person feels betrayed or judged by the therapist who is there to empower the journey of healthy dialogue. It is also the therapist's job to maintain his or her own inner strength and guiding light so that he or she is not consumed by the patient's emotional darkness. Sometimes I wanted to assist him, but thankfully not too often.

Each session was an emotional roller coaster. Sometimes I left the office filled with more anger and resentment, and other times I left with a glimmer of hope that we were making progress, only to leave the next session feeling like my hope was a fantasy that might never be realized.

We continued therapy sessions once a week for two or three months. It became clear that the more I made my wife wrong for pulling away from our marriage and hiring an attorney and feeling like she deceived me, the more complicated and hostile the communication was between us. There were times as my wife was sharing her feelings of fear and anger that I felt our therapist subconsciously sending me a silent signal with a clear message. "If you want to heal your family, save money, and renew your life, you need to surrender and open your heart to feel your wife's suffering, pain, and fears."

Even though I felt justified in my anger, I knew he was right. But all I could hear inside was the voice that said, "What about my suffering, pain, and fears?"

Awakening the Angels

Finally, a few things occurred in therapy that began to open my heart. It started with the simple purity of my wife's tears. I swear that when a woman cries, the angels listen. That is what it felt like in the therapist's room. All the anger I had expressed paled in comparison to my wife's tears. As she tearfully expressed her fears, I looked at our therapist and could see that he sensed her authenticity. And I could see that my soap opera, though good for prime time TV, didn't have a chance in front of a judge. In that sense, the attorney I had divorced was right. We all have our side of the story. It didn't feel fair though! Most men just don't cry well, and when we do, it looks strange since we are usually uncomfortable with our tears and sadness. It reminded me of an old Oscar-winning movie called *Kramer vs. Kramer,* starring Dustin Hoffman and Meryl Streep. It was one of the best movies at the time revealing the complexities of divorce and child custody. Both actors brought the emotional landscape of these turbulent feelings to the big screen, but when Meryl Streep began to cry in the courtroom when confronted by Dustin Hoffman's attorney, even Hoffman's character immediately wanted to protect and defend her. It didn't matter that she requested the divorce and left the marriage and her child. At that moment all the anger, resentment, bitterness, and feelings of revenge disappeared. It is as if the sincere sacredness of a woman's tears tends to cleanse our souls and reconnect us all to our deepest compassion and love. At that moment, a man's innate desire is simply to protect, defend, and forgive, and remember the depth of a love that is never truly lost.

When I was first married, I would have resisted seeing a marriage counselor. Who knows all the reasons we resist certain things when we are young. Pride, stubbornness, and naïveté can all sabotage the learning process. Now these therapy sessions had become the one thing that could possibly save us from drowning. Each time we wrote a check for ninety dollars, I imagined how that was saving thousands more. At times I wondered if all these life lessons were truly going to add to my enrichment, or if I was simply going to become a broken-down old man with broken dreams. It was so easy to slip back into anger and resentment.

Each week I spoke to members of my family, updating them on the divorce process. I knew they could hear the pain in my voice and the weariness of my spirit even when I tried to camouflage that with positive affirmations. Thankfully, they were there for me. I know my dad felt very sad for me, but this time I think even he let go of trying to understand why the second marriage had failed. Some things are simply hard to explain and even harder to fully comprehend.

One of my regrets was that we didn't immediately seek out marriage counseling when we remarried or when the relationship began heading south. I believe it would have given us both a deeper understanding of our interactions. I now highly recommend therapy and relationship seminars to any couple who are pursuing the commitment of intimate relationships.

Chapter 12:

Building a Bridge Across the Fire

As time went on, my heart continued to open and soften, and as mine did, hers opened, as well. Our conversations became more civil as we were able to discuss specific legal aspects of our divorce. Since our son was still a minor at sixteen, child support was necessary. The more understanding and compassionate we were, the easier it was to create a dialogue of fairness. Fairness can appear as a two-headed beast. When there is hostility and distrust, nothing seems fair to either, but when there is benevolence and kindness, fairness can be a practical, essential bridge to obtain the goals you are seeking.

As our dialogue evolved, I became aware that I was still resentful that my wife had an attorney who was coaching and instigating her. I still resented that the cost of that attorney was tunneling its way into our savings, and at times I felt cautious of her motives, knowing that her attorney was still pulling strings in the background attempting to mandate how and what I was suppose to do as a father. I did not need laws outside my own morality to know my own responsibilities and commitment to my children. Though I knew why specific laws were in place for parents, I could feel myself bristle when we discussed child support.

At times there were legal documents presented to me by my wife. It was obvious that her attorney was attempting to manipulate me in any way she could. There were some clauses in these documents that I simply refused to accept and agree to, especially in areas where I was not legally bound. I knew my wife was simply following the authority of her attorney, and in one sense was innocent, but I still did not like it. It just let me know her strings were being pulled by her attorney who was looking out for her interests, not ours. I had to keep reminding myself to follow the path of healing but to continue to have healthy boundaries and to not blink.

As we slowly climbed up the mountain of healing and healthy communication, I knew I could fall off the mountain at any moment, particularly when I felt her attorney was trying to get more from me than was legally justified.

One time when my children were young we were vacationing as a family at Universal Studios in Orlando, Florida. My daughter and I had just gone on the King Kong ride while my wife waited with my son who was about five and too frightened to go. After the ride, Julia, Nathaniel, and I browsed the gift shop allowing their mom to now go on the ride and experience the adventure—and then it happened. I blinked! One moment my eye was on Nathaniel and Julia, and then in an instant Nathaniel was gone. I ran all over looking for him. I felt a gut wrenching fear as I kept screaming his name. A few minutes later, though it seemed like hours, I saw my wife and son coming off the ride. Nathaniel had decided to go on the ride at the last second. My wife thought I knew, and she had no idea what Julia and I had gone through. In one blink, life can change from one road to the other. I knew that our tenuous hold on healing could dissolve in the blink of an eye just as quickly as Nathaniel had disappeared.

I had to stay intensely alert, awake, so as not to lose my foothold. I was still walking through the fire, but the heat seemed to be diminishing some. I prayed I wasn't just getting use to it!

Healing Essentials

Whether healing an illness or emotional wounds, healing is an evolutionary process. Moment by moment it is difficult to see progress, yet when we are true to the process, miracles can occur beyond our expectations.

Without this process, illness becomes worse, emotional wounds become deeper, bitterness grows, and our body and heart become rigid and hard. Sadly, our life's energy diminishes as we adjust and compensate to survive each day.

True healing, however, can not only help us grow but can also become a process of teaching, for when we walk through these fires, and ultimately stand on the other side, sharing what we've learned with others comes naturally. Simply being who you've become serves as an example for others.

The Power of Song and Friends

"Let's record another song," I said again and again until it eventually turned into a fifteen-song CD called "Moments in Time." The process was very healing for my spirit. Some of these songs were written when I was in my early twenties, while others were written in the last few years. Each song was like my child, and it was difficult to leave any behind. These visits with my friend Stu and his wife Janna became a wonderful bonding time for all of us. The fellowship of creativity, music, food, and conversations deepened our relationships with each other, so it was just a matter of time before I heard them say, "We have a friend we'd like you to meet." They knew my divorce was not yet final, but they also understood that my wife and I were not going to reconcile. I didn't think much about it, especially when they said she lived in Michigan.

New Home

After following a realtor around for several months, I finally decided on purchasing a condo that was close to my office. This was the first time in over twenty years that I had lived so close to my office, and could actually go home for lunch. Once again, I felt the simplicity of being single in my new home. My children were doing well. My daughter was to be graduating from college soon, and my son was in his final year of high school. My wife and I were getting closer to finalizing our divorce. I could see a clearing in the distance that I hoped wasn't a fading mirage. I had learned during this process to not blink or take anything for granted, especially since my wife's attorney was still guiding her. That was out of my hands. I had to keep my own vision of healing, maintain healthy communication, and trust in the divine spirit.

Simple Thank You

Sometimes when we left the therapist's office, we each thanked each other. Maybe it was for moments of kindness or compassionate listening, maybe a feeling of being understood, or maybe it was knowing that deep in our hearts neither one of us wanted to intentionally hurt the other person. And for now, that began to feel really good considering the distance we had traveled emotionally.

The Inner Guide

"After you discover deeper compassion, forgiveness, and love, you will want to share this experience with others." I had never forgotten that voice I heard when I asked for guidance during the first divorce. That voice inside became my inner mantra regardless of the storms surrounding me. At times, the voice seemed to echo from a distant canyon. Sometimes it was muffled and distorted from the turbulence of anger and confusion, but still the voice called me forward to let go and surrender.

Surrender is a paradox to the thinking mind. In a war, the last thing we want to do is surrender, admit defeat, and lose everything. It is difficult to surrender when you believe you are justified in your actions and right in your beliefs. In the end, we can find ourselves bitter, hardened, and cut off from meaningful relationships. Don't we all know someone who has simply detached from a loved one or even a family member? Without realizing it, we can become prisoners in a prison of our own design. After a while, the extraordinariness of who we are can be reduced to someone who has forgotten how to give and receive love. Compassion and forgiveness remain words we hear at church or temple, yet we are unable to authentically integrate the experience of these virtues into our daily life.

At the time, I understood the art of surrender did not mean losing at all. It meant letting go of what was in the way of achieving the goals I truly desired, and even more important to reconnect to my own authentic spirit, wisdom, and compassion. The last thing I wanted was to be someone who was afraid to love, guarded by emotional wounds that never truly healed. Ideally, I wanted to bring a landscape of learning to my relationships that would allow me to love more deeply and to receive someone else's love more graciously. At that time, though, I was just trying to get through the day without a panic attack.

Once again my friend Michael encouraged me to write this story and to teach this message. "The story is even more powerful now," he said, almost as if I was purposely collecting data for an inspiring novel. But I was not ready, not nearly. Writing this story was the farthest thing from my mind. I was healing, and at that moment, the last thing I wanted to do was share this story. You cannot inspire others when you are not feeling inspired.

Each morning when I awoke, I imagined this was all a dream—that I was happily married and had never been divorced. Life was simple, successful, and joyous. But then reality hit and the remaining fog of the dream disappeared into vapors. Thankfully, the therapy sessions were creating movement, and we were getting closer to another finalized divorce, but, of course, that was just the beginning of another new life, one of many lifetimes in this one life. I wondered what the Master Spirit had in store for me as I continued to allow myself to surrender, face all my fears, and open to my creative heart.

Chapter 13:
Being Open to What We Truly Want

My friend Steven asked me, "Would you want to be with your soul mate at this time?" I nonchalantly said I just want to have fun. He continued, "But if you met just the right person, would you want that at this time?" As I hedged his question, I realized I was always looking for the "right" person. Regardless of how many blind dates, brief romantic encounters, and comfortable relationships I've had, I have always been a romantic wanting to be a prince for my princess. But I have also always wanted the initial passion to remain, grow, and last forever. It has taken me years to learn the essential ingredients to manifest that possibility. It seems so simple, yet I was a living example of how easy it was to fall from grace and become a disenchanted romantic. I was still learning, and thankfully, I was still willing to learn with an open heart and an open spirit.

Final Sessions

The last few sessions ironed out issues related to child support, financial obligations, and once again, the division of valuables. I was glad we were moving forward and finalizing important agreements. Going through divorce twice, I was able to see the absurdity of couples fighting over small matters when they are married. I remembered times I was upset if money was spent on something I didn't believe was necessary. But then when two people divorce, they need two homes, two beds, and two separate bank accounts, two of everything.

I knew that being divorced was going to create more financial stress, but at least we were avoiding bankruptcy. Somehow putting things in perspective made me feel better. However much money this divorce was costing, it was far less than it would have been if I hadn't divorced my divorce attorney. Every time we gave our therapist ninety dollars, I thought that it was the best ninety dollars we could spend. We agreed to divide the final bill from my wife's attorney. Divorce was certainly not the way to create financial wealth and stability. For hardworking, average-income people, it could be a tremendous financial setback, not to mention financial disaster.

In our last session, our therapist had us face each other and share whatever we wished to share with the other person. The mood was somber and calm. Even though our business there was ending, we knew that regardless of our relationship with each other that our partnership with our children would be ongoing. We both deeply understood how our relationship also affected our children. Thankfully, we were able to share positive things with each other as we sat one last time in that room, which had been more like a boxing ring for our ongoing sparring.

Ultimately, we most appreciated who we were as a mother and father for our children. Our children had weathered the storms of these divorces and had become stronger and wiser, even though we were all still mending our wounds. "Thank you for being the mother of our children." "Thank you for battling it out here in this office rather than letting others control our lives." "Thank you for sharing." "I'm sorry I hurt you." "Thank you for your tears." These were some of the words that were exchanged. As comforting as these words were, there was still the pain. I felt the relief of a marathon runner finally finishing the race though I was emotionally and physically exhausted. I remember our therapist asking, "Is there anything more either of you want to say?" That night I wished I had heard some additional words to ease some of my mending wounds. But that is why our own healing is so essential. Others are not responsible for our inner spiritual journey. That night was perfect just as it was. Before we left that evening, we thanked our therapist for his wisdom and inner guidance and for not having a heart attack while we were slugging it out. Though there were still healthy, protective boundaries between my wife and I, we were able to embrace before we left. It was sincere.

For the first time, I began to see the possibility of these two people discovering a new friendship, like I was observing my wife and me from a distance. Not that long ago, I had no desire to be friends ever again, but that is what can occur with healing. No agenda, no manipulation, no controlling—we simply let go and allowed the healing experience to take us to a new land with fresh possibilities. I continued to hear my inner chant: deeper love, compassion, forgiveness, sharing with others, sharing with others. The fire below my feet almost began to feel soothing, like hot sand on a summer day.

First Meeting

"What are you doing Saturday night?" he said over the phone. "Remember that friend of ours we told you about? Well, she's in town. Why don't you come over tomorrow night, and we can play music and go out for dinner?" My schedule was free so the answer was easy. "What time?"

Another blind date. Of course, I will be kind and charming and make it through the evening. Of course, this was a friend of Stu and Janna, so I hoped the evening went well, and everyone was happy by the end of the night. I had gone on enough blind dates to be comfortable with the process. The first time I waited for a blind date in a restaurant, my body reacted positively or negatively to every person who came through the door. It was nerve racking wondering what the person was going to look like. After several blind dates, I began to relax and simply enjoy the person regardless of circumstances. Sometimes I knew within 15 seconds that this was the last date we would have, and I imagined the other person felt the same way.

She greeted me at the back door of my friend's house as I opened the screen. She said her name was Julie, and went to shake my hand. I instinctively reached to give her a gentle hug and felt her warmly receive it without any hesitation. I heard the voices in my mind immediately assess the encounter. "She is nice, cute, playful, about my age, great smile, healthy body—should be an interesting evening." I didn't feel sparks fly, but we were on the same playing field, and the night was just beginning.

Signing Papers

As I signed the papers and wrote out the final check to my now ex-wife's attorney, it was official—not a time of celebration but relief. Once again, we were legally divorced. Thankfully, we had avoided the courtroom and a financial ruin disaster. It had cost less than twenty thousand dollars, a hefty sum regardless. But, when you have been staring down the barrel of bankruptcy, it feels great to have survived and to feel healthy enough to move forward.

I knew our relationship with each other would evolve with time and be shaped from our continued communication and healing. Our children were still our common bond, and our commitment to their well being and their future would always remain a constant priority for both of us. My vision for our family was that once again we could celebrate holidays and family time together. How complicated divorce makes things when children have to schedule separate times with parents who never want to see each other. As children become adults, it can be exhausting trying to please each parent who may be demanding of their time. Life is complicated enough! In each divorce, my children were always my inspirational guides. In spite of the divorces both their mom and I wanted them to always be connected to the sacredness of our family. Yes, it was different, but it was real, it was ours, and the expression of our love never stopped.

Yes, There Is a Reason

I have learned that many people remarry their ex-spouse for various reasons. Some of them include the realization that they truly made a mistake and that all relationships have issues to work through, financial stability, or reuniting the family. Or once two people have been apart they realize that they have more in common than they thought and do, indeed, love each other deeply. After a short time though, like us, some find themselves facing another divorce while others seem to work through their glitches and discover a healthy compromise and acceptance with each other.

Yet when we are truly healing and evolving through the complexities of divorce, we inevitably find lessons, understanding, and blessings. When I look back I can clearly see that we needed to be married again to realize that the love we had for each other was deep, tender, and true, but it was no longer the love of lovers. It had become the love of committed friends that ultimately would always be there for each other. It has been hard to understand let alone explain to others that love can take many forms. It is easy to be confused when the passion diminishes but not the caring. I believe we both knew this, perhaps subconsciously, but we were willing to try. We hoped that maybe if we worked hard enough at it, the fires would be turned on again. At first it seemed like a possibility as the initial flame of our excitement brought new light into our lives, but then the flame slowly retreated, until the light turned back into shadows.

When we were first divorced, each of the women I was with would say, "Maybe you and your ex-wife should get back together again. After all, you are such wonderful friends." Even my dad would make the same suggestion since he had never seen two divorced people be so involved in each other's lives. But we all have our own journey.

Not of all us go in a straight line to get somewhere. Many like myself go on roads less traveled as if we are being guided by invisible hands. Now that the fog from the second divorce has cleared, my ex-wife and I can move freely forward in our lives. New partners need not be anxious about our committed friendship and partnership we share for our children. I did not think I would be friends again with my ex-wife after the second divorce, but that is the beauty and the mystery of our growing and healing. My ex-wife will always be the wonderful mother to our children.

In essence, this is an uncommon love story. It is filled with anger, grief, rage, frustration, and fear, and yet it is also filled with compassion, forgiveness, love, and transformation. It is my story, yet the lessons of this journey can be applied to your own lives. It is essential to understand the cost of neglecting healing or simply failing to understand the healing journey. We can become bankrupt not only financially but in something more essential—our spirit. So this uncommon love story about healing our families, saving a fortune, and re-newing our lives can become a guiding light in your life. That is my vision and my sincere desire and commitment.

I am thankful for my ex-wife as our friendship continues to evolve and heal. Some of the words I wanted to hear that last night in the therapist's office have been expressed over time. It's not so much the words but the feeling that vibrates through our sincere apologies and acts of forgiveness. Our children are extraordinary, living fully and pursuing their passions. We all continue to communicate in person, phone, email, and even Face book. On holidays we celebrate together and continue to be with each other as often as possible. I have the best ex-wife. She is a dear friend. And I have the greatest children. I am blessed!

We Never Know What's Next

I was not anticipating the magic of the evening. I remember Stu asking me, "What do you think about Julie?" after my new blind date and his wife Janna went off in another direction in the restaurant. I said, "She is really special."

After dinner we all headed back to my friend's home and sat around for hours playing music and sharing stories. The evening had a magical quality to it, something I was not expecting, especially since I was newly single and not necessarily looking for a serious relationship. The hours went quickly as we sat talking way into the night. I remembered my friend Steve's question, "But if your soul mate came along, would you let go of the notion that you just wanted to have fun being single?" A few weeks later I was speaking to my brother on the phone, and he asked if I was dating anyone yet. It shocked me when I said, "I think I met my soul mate." Those were sacred words, words I hardly used in my life referring to a new relationship. Life was beginning to feel brand new, and my heart was welcoming new adventures. I felt very alive!

Learning from the Past and Starting New

It was hard to believe as we sat in a relationship seminar that my new sweetheart Julie and I had been together almost one year. We were not there because something was wrong, but because we knew how easy relationships could fall apart. We were choosing to grow in healthy ways with each other, and most important, learn how to communicate with open minds and hearts. In my younger years, I would have resisted a seminar like the one we were attending, especially if I had thought that "everything was fine." Regardless of what the future held for us, I knew we were beginning our relationship the right way.

As we sat in the room, I looked around at the other twelve couples. We were in our honeymoon phase, excited and loving throughout the weekend. Of course, most of us in that room understood that honeymoons can end, and sadly, relationships can dissolve. The majority of the other couples were facing difficult times. The weariness and anger was easy to observe. Some couples were there hoping to rekindle a spark in their relationship; others were looking for anything that might save a drowning partnership. I knew the look and the feeling well. My sweetheart and I have continued to use many of the communication tools we learned from that seminar, and remind each other of the importance of mutual respect, trust, healthy communication, mutual admiration, and shared visions and dreams.

We Are Family

Though it is impossible to "see" time, we can observe the changes that occur as time passes. Sometimes we do not like what we see; other times we feel blessed and thankful. This was one of those times, the beginning of many family gatherings.

My children and ex-wife had met my sweetheart before, but as we sat enjoying our brunch on that spring day, it was evident we were a family. What seemed impossible a few years ago now felt wonderful, intimate, and normal. My daughter who was living and working in Boston was home for the weekend, while my son would soon be setting out on an adventure traveling to Hawaii. I was so proud of them both knowing how much they had grown individually through the years and who they were now as adults. My ex-wife and my sweetheart appreciated and liked each other. I was not surprised. As I looked around the table, I could deeply see each person's unique greatness, compassion, integrity, and love. As we shared food, stories, and laughter, it mirrored the healing and commitment of our amazing journey. We had each become stronger and healthier from the lessons of our lives. I realized how blessed I was. Like the blossoming seeds of spring, we were all being reborn with exciting new visions for the future.

People often ask me, "How do I stop repeating the cycle of painful relationships? How do I keep myself from becoming bitter and disenchanted?" That is what this story and my fire walk have been about. When we learn these healing lessons, our hearts continues to open to greater love, forgiveness, and compassion. In essence, we all must learn to give what we truly want. If you want love, give love. If you want healthy communication, practice healthy communication. If you desire passion and tenderness, give passion and tenderness. If you want respect and honesty, give these qualities. Discover the people in your life who also desire to learn and heal from their own past.

Learn to listen within to the voice inside. "In your deepest anger and rage, you will discover even deeper love and compassion, and when you do, you will share these healing lessons with others." I have never forgotten those words or that moment when my life was falling apart. Like a mantra, those words are my sacred companion everyday, always reminding who I want to be for my children, my ex-wife, my sweetheart, my friends, my family, and this world. I am thankful and blessed to share this story with you.

EPILOGUE

Months ago Marty had emailed me the manuscript for his revised book about our healing divorces and asked me to read it and give whatever feedback—both positive and negative. I dutifully printed out the manuscript and put it into a folder putting it in my stack of "to do's." Time passed. Actually months passed and whenever he asked me about it, I always had some excuse mixed in with the real reason. I just could not go there into all that pain and review and relive those hard times again. It was just too painful, too heavy and I could not find the emotional energy required to complete the task.

I felt guilty about not responding to his gentle nudges for I knew that he wanted to be honest, respectful and forthright about publishing our story. Also I knew he had worked hard and dug deep within himself, since the writing of this story demanded it of him. So, why could I not pony up the courage to at least read it and respond appropriately?

The day finally arrived when he said, "Ok, this is it. It is going to the publishers next week. So this is your last chance." The fire underneath me began to flame hotter. Could I really fully endorse this book knowing that I had missed the opportunity to tell the readers, that this is truly what happened, as far as his side of the story? Yes, we are now "life friends" not XX's and we share a common commitment to stay healthy in our relationship with each other. Not for the sake of our children, but for our sakes. We can't be whole in our current intimate relationships until we heal our wounds and make peace with each other and our past. And, of course, forgive ourselves and all of it.

Marty and I had for the last couple of years shared a ritual of meeting for brunch on Father's and Mother's Day. With our children both grown and newly out of the nest and both out of state, this was our way of holding the space of our nuclear family. Parenthood has always been our sacred space and I know that every time we celebrate and honor one another that it continues to help us heal and solidify our family ties even though we have both moved on in life. Interestingly, because his sweetheart was traveling out of town with work and family commitments, he and I found ourselves having Father's day, just the two of us.

I don't know why I brought the manuscript to the restaurant, maybe to prove to Marty my good intentions about reading it and following through. I was grasping for whatever impetus or thrust I could grab on to, so that I could inch my way toward the "big read." Like most people I tend to avoid pain and avoid it being triggered. The night before we met for brunch, I did pick up the first chapter and read it. It hit a piece of the past that caused me to literally cry out aloud and laugh both equally and tearfully together. Then I slammed down the rest of the pages and retreated into the next room breathing deeply and self soothing myself as I had been instructed to do in therapy.

What occurred that next day when we met for our ritual Father's day brunch, was absolutely extraordinary, liberating and even more healing than I could ever have imagined and had always hoped for. After we ate, he came over to my home and we took turns and read our story out loud to each other. It was a gift for each of us. Divorcing Marty the second time was a bigger loss for me than the first time. I felt as though I was divorcing my best friend for life. The impact was emotionally devastating. My silent prayer was that somehow, some way, we could heal ourselves, our children, and re-establish a new friendship and keep our family bond. I wanted and needed atonement.

I have so much gratitude for the love and the challenging journey Marty has accomplished and brought forward in this book. It is a blessing when I hear from others, their amazement and delight about our current friendship and how we manage our life as a family. Now, we have all gone separate paths, however, our family roots have grown very deep and are continually fed by our love. This is what I know is truth for us. We will always remain connected. My sincere and heartfelt hope is that our story serves as an inspiration to all.

Kathryn

A GUIDED OUTLINE
FOR HEALING THROUGH
DIVORCE AND "HAVE THE RELATIONSHIPS YOU
DESIRE."

Thank you for reading "Divorce, An Uncommon Love Story." As you continue to explore the journey of your own healing, become familiar with the specific laws in your state regarding divorce. There are many excellent books and insightful and practical information that can be downloaded from the internet.

Exercise:
>   Begin to write out a vision of how you would like your life to look like two years from now. Imagine your life being fully expressed and extraordinary in the areas of: new relationships, career, finances, children and family, emotional, spiritual, and physical health. Everyday remind yourself of that vision.

Thoughts That Already Exist About Divorce That Can Add To Our Suffering:

1. Feelings of failure
2. I am not good enough
3. I cannot ever be happy and fulfilled
4. Feeling rejected and guilty
5. Feelings of embarrassment
6. Feeling unworthy of being loved
7. Children will suffer painful consequences in a divorce
8. Failing as a parent for our children

9. Needing to protect yourself and hire an attorney quickly
10. Divorce is sinful
11. Feelings of being a bad person
12. Divorce is normally mean spirited

Exercise:

> Remember a time in your life that was difficult and stressful in which it seemed impossible for something good to manifest, yet it did! Sometimes the most painful moments in our lives can contribute to our greatest insights, triumphs, healing, and spiritual transformation. Think about what you did, and what actions you took.

How Do You Think You Contributed To The Relationship Not Working? Too often we do not observe our own actions and non-actions and how it affects the relationship we are in.

1. Perhaps you stopped communicating what you were feeling
2. Perhaps you stopped listening to the other person's feelings
3. Perhaps you had patterns of making the other person wrong
4. Perhaps you were controlling, dominating, or manipulating
5. Perhaps you acted like a victim and made your partner and yourself wrong

What Are Your Greatest Fears Regarding Divorce?

1. Perhaps the fear of the unknown

2.   Perhaps   the   fear   of   what   other
people may think
3.   Perhaps the fear of being alone
4.   Perhaps   the   fear   of   losing   your
children
5.   Perhaps the fear of change
6.   Perhaps the fear of financial loss
7.   Perhaps the fear of failing
8.   Perhaps   the   fear   of   physical,   and   emotional
instability

Exercise:
    Write down what you feel angry about:
    I am angry that_____

Where do you feel the anger in your body?

Exercise:
    Write down what you feel sad about:
    I am sad that _____

Where do you feel the sadness in your body?

Exercise:
    Write   down   the   qualities   and   aspects   of   your
    relationship that you enjoyed:
What   I   enjoyed   about   our   relationship
was_____

Exercise:
    Write down how you feel that person contributed to
    your life:
How   that   person   contributed   to   my   life
was_____

Exercise:
> Write down what you forgive yourself for:
> I forgive myself for_____

Exercise:
> Write down what you forgive your partner for:
> I forgive my partner for_____

Exercise:
> Write down what you have learned about yourself
> What   I   have   learned   about   myself
> is_____

Exercise:
> Write down what you appreciate about yourself
> What   I   appreciate   about   myself
> is_____

Exercise:
> Write down five qualities you desire most in a relationship.

Motivating Factors to Create Healing:

1. Survival, protection, keeping and saving money
2. Avoiding a life of bitterness and anger
3. Personal power—I know I am going to make it
4. Seeing the possibility of a healthy environment for your children and each other as your heart begins to feel compassion
5. Seeing the possibility of communicating powerfully, and lovingly with your partner
6. Feeling the power of healing yourself in your own spiritual growth and connection with a higher power

7.   Knowing that the power of your own healing brings light and love and new possibilities for other people, and the world we live in.

Affirmation: I am now willing to move forward in my life to fulfill my vision for a healthy abundant future. The specific action steps I am now committed to are:

1. Enrolling in a personal growth seminar or workshop
2. Seeing a therapist to learn more about myself
3. Learning or doing something new to re-create my life
4. Learning to dance or play a musical instrument
5. Writing down specific goals to accomplish my dreams
6. Creating wellness strategies in my life

ABOUT THE AUTHOR

Dr. Marty Finkelstein has been a holistic chiropractor since 1980 specializing in physical, and emotional healing and wellness. He has hosted, "To Your Health" a cable television show, and "Wake Up To Your Health" an Atlanta radio show.

He has been the chiropractic representative for Flying Doctors of America where he has teamed with medical doctors, dentists, and other health care professionals providing services to thousands of people in Mexico, Peru, and The Dominican Republic. Dr. Finkelstein is a motivational educator who inspires others to greater wellness and healing in their lives. He is the creator of several workshops including "Healing Through Separation and Divorce" and "Have the Relationships You Desire."

Dr. Finkelstein is also the author of:

If Relationships Were Like Sports, Men Would At Least Know The Score
8 Lessons For Life On Hole 1
A Life Of Wellness
The Seven Gifts
Moments Of Time—A CD of 15 original songs

Dr. Marty Finkelstein has an office in Decatur, and Conyers, Georgia

To order additional copies of:

DIVORCE, AN UNCOMMON LOVE STORY

Write to:

Dr. Marty Finkelstein
4292 suite D Memorial drive
Decatur, Georgia, 30032

Or Email drmarty3@yahoo.com
www.mydecaturchiropractor.com

Dr. Marty Finkelstein is available for speaking engagements, workshops, and seminars to assist others through divorce, and discovering how to manifest new healthy relationships in their lives.

Books can also be ordered through Amazon, and all major bookstores

CPSIA information can be obtained at www.ICGtesting.com
230456LV00001B/37/P.

9 781602 646773